30-SECOND
OPERA

30-SECOND
OPERA

THE 50 CRUCIAL CONCEPTS, ROLES AND PERFORMERS,
EACH EXPLAINED IN HALF A MINUTE

Consultant Editor
Hugo Shirley

Foreword
Kasper Holten

Contributors
John Allison
Rupert Christiansen
George Hall
Cormac Newark
Anna Picard
Hugo Shirley
Alexandra Wilson

Illustrations
Ivan Hissey

IVY PRESS

This paperback edition published in the UK in 2019 by
Ivy Press
An imprint of The Quarto Group
The Old Brewery, 6 Blundell Street
London N7 9BH, United Kingdom
T (0)20 7700 6700 **F** (0)20 7700 8066
www.QuartoKnows.com

First published in hardback in 2015

British Library Cataloguing-in-
Publication Data
A catalogue record for this
book is available from the
British Library.

ISBN: 978-1-78240-756-0

This book was conceived,
designed and produced by
Ivy Press
58 West Street, Brighton, BN1 2RA, UK

Creative Director **Peter Bridgewater**
Publisher **Susan Kelly**
Editorial Director **Tom Kitch**
Art Director **Michael Whitehead**
Editor **Jamie Pumfrey**
Designer **Ginny Zeal**
Glossaries Text **Hugo Shirley**
Commissioning Editor **Stephanie Evans**

Printed in Slovenia by GPS Group

10 9 8 7 6 5 4 3 2 1

CONTENTS

FOREWORD
Kasper Holten

The idea of taking what is one of the world's most
complicated art forms, one which is (in)famous for taking its time, and trying
to say something meaningful about it in 30-second bites, is as wonderfully
absurd as the idea of opera itself. Irresistible, in other words, just like opera.

And yet, again just like opera, maybe the idea makes a lot of sense when
you look at it more closely. Opera stands apart because it is not
really an art form in itself, rather a composite of all the other art forms – the
world's first 'multi-medium'. Opera speaks directly to us, but there's
a lot to be learned from the many building blocks that combine to bring
it alive: its musical history, context and language, its composers,
characters and performers. Producing opera on the grand scale often feels
like being a chef, preparing a 15-course meal. And knowledge of the different
ingredients and the ways in which they complement one another, can help in
the full appreciation of this long and lavish feast.

Opera is a series of paradoxes: it is and was originally intended as a form
of entertainment. Yet it also offers us a true and profound understanding
of human beings and of how people interact in a way no other art form can
really do. Certain scenarios might seem completely silly, meaningless or over
the top, although maybe exactly in its portrayal of the very stuff of life lies
opera's deepest attraction: it is hard to explain why we need it, but clearly we
do – thanks in part to modern technology more people listen to opera now
than ever before in its 400-year history.

By combining theatre and music, and harnessing the unique power of the
unamplified human voice, opera offers us a language for those situations
where words alone fail us: the emotional highs and lows, the irrational
aspects of our existence, the contrast between the intimacy of our private,
inner worlds and the public stage. It isn't necessary to understand the
language to see, hear and be utterly affected by characters whose voices
express the emotions that touch everyone – from unbridled joy, passion,
love, loss, jealousy and anger to the more subtle conveyance of sadness,
loneliness, hope and disappointment.

In a well-intentioned bid to introduce new people to opera, the experts often start out by telling them the whole story of the opera they are about to see, robbing them of any kind of suspense. I have always felt this was a shame, and it is my hope that this book can offer a different approach to learning about opera – one that will appeal in equal measure to newcomers and those who want to gain a deeper knowledge and understanding of the art form. By lifting the curtain on the various elements of opera and the ways in which the genre has evolved since its early inception, *30-Second Opera* opens up a more informed way to listen, to understand, and above all to enjoy your experience of a performance.

Of course, 30 seconds can never exhaust any aspect of opera – or of anything for that matter. And yet if the mere half minute it takes to read one of these topics can encourage you to experience opera for the first time or make you listen in a slightly different way the next time you spend six hours on Wagner's *Parsifal*, then surely those 30 seconds will have been more than worth it.

Kasper Holten
DIRECTOR OF OPERA 2011–2017
ROYAL OPERA HOUSE, COVENT GARDEN

INTRODUCTION
Hugo Shirley

Doctor Johnson, no fan of opera, once described
the art form as 'an exotic and irrational entertainment'. Any opera fan
would counter that it's exactly those characteristics – just two among
many – that they love about it; others might still initially find its foreign
languages and strange conventions puzzling. Part of the aim of this book,
however, is to embrace opera's exoticness and irrationality, to revel in its
complexities – to resist the temptation to explain it away in terms of its
similarities to other art forms.

Because opera in itself shouldn't need defending, and although it
takes elements from the other arts, it is unique. Its history and its often
contested relationship with society as a whole, meanwhile, is part of what
makes it so fascinating, as does the fact that its central tension between
music and words makes for a near-impossible creative balancing act –
there's barely a handful of operas that one could describe as 'perfect'.

By a similar token, operas often contain too much to be consumed at
one sitting. There are plenty of details one can miss first time around – or
even the tenth – but don't let that worry you: this is one of the reasons
opera fans keep coming back for more. Another is the remarkable power
of the unamplified human voice singing some of the greatest music ever
written, and it's not always necessary to hear the words or understand the
intricacies of the plot to infer the emotional content, as the widespread
use of opera in broader culture demonstrates.

Unlike other introductions-to opera, *30-Second Opera* offers a means
of getting to know the subject at whatever pace, in whatever order and
in whatever quantities the reader wants. Its 50 topics in seven sections
cannot possibly cover every single aspect of the art form, but they will
allow the reader to start compiling his or her own picture of it, or, in the
case of those already familiar with opera, to flesh out the picture they
already have. The fact that this isn't just a collection of opera plots or
composer biographies means that we've been able to focus on ideas, on
what it is that makes different operas and composers so fascinating and

important. We also take care to suggest examples to listen to or watch, which now – thanks to the likes of YouTube and Spotify – are rarely more than a mouse-click away.

Each of the sections here has its own glossary as well as a profile of a key performer from throughout opera's history. **Building Blocks** considers the very architecture and institutions that opera relies on to exist, as well as the essential elements that make up an opera – the music, the words, the performers. **Words & Music** delves in deeper, detailing the forms in which those elements are traditionally presented. **History** offers a concise account of how opera has developed from its beginnings to the present day, taking into account its relationship to society as a whole, its role within different national cultures and its interplay – particularly since the beginning of the twentieth century – with technology. In this

third section, we have retained terms such as 'Baroque', 'Classical' and 'Romantic' for the sake of familiarity, even if such traditional categories suggest the sort of neat historical pigeon-holing that opera's unruly, unpredictable story seeks at every opportunity to resist.

Genres, the fourth section, outlines some of the different types of opera that have existed throughout its history – including the serious and the comic, the grand and the tragic – while **Key Composers** gathers together 12 of the most significant composers of opera throughout its history. Regrettably, some great opera composers have had to be excluded, but the section covers most of the operas that one might encounter in the opera house today, as well as considering the existence of different national schools of opera.

Voices explains in more detail the many sorts of singers required in opera, from *coloratura soprano* to *basso profondo* and everything in between, while the final section, **Characters**, explores some of the recognizable archetypes one might find in opera throughout the centuries, and what they can be understood to represent. These characters, and the terms of reference of many of the other chapters, perhaps inevitably centre around what is referred to as the 'long nineteenth century', the period roughly from the French Revolution to the outbreak of the First World War, in which opera and its institutions became established in the way that they persist in the twenty-first century.

In some respects, the greatest challenge facing opera today is to reconcile that tradition with the necessities – financial, social and artistic – of the modern world. This book, I hope, reflects that, while also – through the passion, knowledge and humour of its contributors – making it clear what opera has to offer us today and into the future. I hope, too, that it might play a small role in persuading new audiences that opera can speak to them and to everybody – that it won't bite, even that it just might, if you give it a chance, grab hold of you and never let go.

ORPHÉE

BUILDING BLOCKS

articulation Composers can use curved lines over groups of notes in a score to show which notes they want joined together in a phrase, and, in the cases of sung lines, where they want breaths to be taken – instructions that are not always followed to the letter.

cadenza Italian for cadence. A cadence in its simplest sense denotes a standard end of the phrase as signalled by a pair of chords that were understood as serving as musical punctuation. From the earliest operas, it became traditional for singers to apply ornaments to important cadences. These 'cadenzas' – sometimes improvised, but in later operas also written into the score – provided a singer with a chance to show off (often including exciting top notes). Such apparently flippant practices were largely abandoned as the nineteenth century progressed, and were never widely permitted in German opera.

continuo Continuo (or, more correctly, 'Basso continuo') refers to the process of turning a straightforward bass line into a fully fledged harmonic accompaniment. From the very earliest operas this would be improvised by a variety of instruments, but in later Baroque and classical repertoire, this would consist of a keyboard instrument (usually a harpsichord, but also on occasion an early piano called the *fortepiano*) and sometimes a cello and would be most audible in the recitative between arias.

da capo Italian musical instruction meaning literally 'from [the] head', placed at the end of a piece, which dictates that it should be repeated 'da capo'. In opera, it most frequently occurred in the Baroque period (and especially in Handel). In 'da capo arias', as they are often called, the singer performs the first section of an aria without ornamentation first time around, before, after the second section, offering a repeat of the first section, which gives them a chance to ornament the line to their heart's content. It might not make dramatic sense, but can offer the opportunity for impressive vocal fireworks.

diva Translating literally as 'goddess' (the male equivalent is 'divo'), the word diva reflects the importance opera-lovers attached to stars from the very earliest period in opera; the fact that this word (along with 'prima donna' – meaning, literally, 'first lady') is also current today in other musical contexts suggests how little celebrity culture has changed.

dynamics The relative loudness of specific notes and phrases on different instruments or in different voices were specified in the score by the use of dynamic markings: *piano* (*p*) meant quiet, *forte* (*f*) loud; *mezzo-piano* (*mp* or 'half-quiet') and *mezzo-forte* (*mf* or 'half-loud') offered degrees in between; *fortissimo* (*ff*) or *pianissimo* (*pp*). Additional dynamic markings include *crescendo* and *diminuendo* for gradually becoming either louder or softer, as well as accents.

messa di voce Not to be confused with *mezza voce* ('half voice', which describes singing quietly), *messa di voce* is Italian for 'placing the voice' and describes the technique of going from soft to loud and back to soft on a particular note. It's a device that requires great skill to execute, since the natural tendency is to go sharp (above the note) as volume is increased and flat (below the note) as it is decreased.

notation The term applied to the way music is written down on the page of score. Throughout history, the extent to which music has been notated has depended on many different factors: in early operas, when the composer was low in the pecking order, notation's function was to provide only the most basic instructions of what was to be performed, giving the performers space to build their own interpretation. During the nineteenth century, the 'score' became increasingly important, with notation increasingly specific.

phrase As in spoken language, an aria or a musical line can normally be separated into a series of phrases that make musical sense on their own – and which in singing are usually dictated by the performer's breathing. There are also conventional ways of phrasing – of shaping a musical phrase – that are part and parcel of performing traditional opera: for example, portamento (artfully executed slides between certain notes) is essential in the idiomatic performance of nineteenth-century Italian repertoire. See **articulation**.

regietheater Pronounced 'ray-jee-tay-ar-ter' and deriving from the German word meaning, roughly, 'director's theatre', *Regietheater* refers to a style of staging opera in which the director emphasizes one or other aspect of the work in question or, on occasion, imposes their own *Konzept* (the German word is often used, not without a hint of derision, to imply disapproval). In some ways originating in Marxist stagings in post-war East Germany, the practice arguably goes back to early pragmatic attempts to reinterpret the near-impossible scenic demands of Wagner's operas. One of the most controversial aspects of modern opera, it also reflects the need to rethink and reinterpret repertoire staples, to present the exhibits in the 'operatic museum' in a different light.

LIBRETTO

the 30-second opera

The words for an opera – which are given the Italian term libretto (little book) – are usually supplied by a professional librettist, although a few composers have written their own, notably Wagner. During opera's earlier history, particularly admired librettos – such as those by Metastasio – were set by numerous different composers; later it became the norm for each opera to have its own libretto. The librettist usually supplied the text before the composer started to write the music, although typically a composer would request changes once composition was underway. Composers often worked regularly with the same librettist (as Mozart did with Da Ponte) or team of librettists. These relationships had a master-servant dynamic although some, including Verdi's contrasting partnerships with Piave and Boito, were more equal. Occasionally a librettist would invent a scenario from scratch but most used pre-existing literary texts, especially plays: there have, for instance, been many Shakespearean operas. The librettist's job was to put the original text into verse (although some later composers set 'prose librettos') and make numerous cuts. Composers could not simply set a play to music unaltered because text takes far longer to deliver when sung rather than spoken, and operas often involve a great deal of textual repetition.

3-SECOND MOTIF
The libretto is the text of an opera; it includes stage directions as well as the words that the performers sing.

3-MINUTE ARIA
For much of opera's history, librettos had to be approved by the theatre and municipal authorities before they could be set. Censors wielded great power, especially in Italy, and could instruct librettists to alter their texts on religious, moral or political grounds: many texts for Verdi's operas were subjected to cuts. Librettos were rarely 'fixed texts' and were frequently bowdlerized when performed in cities beyond that of the first performance.

RELATED TOPICS
See also
SCORE
page 18

THE ARIA
page 38

THE RECITATIVE
page 40

3-SECOND BIOGRAPHIES
'METASTASIO' (PIETRO ANTONIO DOMENICO TRAPASSI)
1698–1782
Italian poet and author of numerous *opera seria* libretti

LORENZO DA PONTE
1749–1838
Italian librettist, remembered for his comic operas for Mozart

FRANCESCO MARIA PIAVE
1810–76
Italian librettist of many of Verdi's famous operas

30-SECOND TEXT
Alexandra Wilson

One of opera's great partnerships: librettist Hugo von Hofmannsthal and composer Richard Strauss.

HUGO HOFMANNSTHAL
ARIADNE AUF NAXOS
MIT FARBIGEN ORIGINAL-STEINDRUCKEN
VON
WILLI NOWAK
VERLAG DER MAREES-GESELLSCHAFT / R. PIPER & CO.
OUVERTURE
zur Oper
Fidelio
LUDWIG VAN BEETHOVEN
Op. 72b.

SCORE

the 30-second opera

The score is the document where

a composer writes down the music of an opera on a stave, allowing it to be reproduced. A full score contains the notes the singers sing and those the orchestra plays, together with indications of tempo, dynamics and articulation. However, the degree to which composers have stipulated these has varied. In the seventeenth and eighteenth centuries, composers notated few performance directions since they were usually present to supervise the first performance; furthermore, improvisation was an accepted and expected part of operatic performance. In the nineteenth century, the score gradually came to be seen as a more fixed 'work', which performers were expected to follow closely: Rossini, for example, began the practice of writing out the (previously improvised) cadenzas. Nevertheless, singers continued to take liberties, inserting arias of their choosing, particularly into Italian operas, where there was more acceptance of cuts, interpolations and performer freedom than in, say, the German tradition. From the later twentieth century, scores were followed more scrupulously. Recent decades have seen the rise of scholarly critical editions, which attempt to present the music as the composer intended it, omitting editorial changes and performance conventions that have built up over time.

RELATED TOPICS
See also
LIBRETTO
page 16

THE OVERTURE
page 36

THE RECITATIVE
page 40

ENSEMBLE
page 46

3-SECOND MOTIF
Composers usually notate the essential melodic and harmonic structure of an opera in short score format before fleshing out the full orchestration.

3-MINUTE ARIA
From the later nineteenth century onwards, composers began to write detailed instructions in their scores about how a scene should look on stage and how singers should act: Wagner, Strauss and Puccini were notably specific in this regard. Somewhat paradoxically, these instructions about staging are nowadays rarely observed, despite the fact that most productions and conductors treat a composer's *musical* instructions with considerable reverence.

3-SECOND BIOGRAPHY
GIULIO RICORDI
1840–1912
Italian publisher who took over the family firm, Casa Ricordi, in Milan in 1863, bringing out the scores of many of Verdi's later works and helping to lure him out of retirement to compose *Otello* and *Falstaff*

30-SECOND TEXT
Alexandra Wilson

Contemporary critical fashion calls for a return to the original author's musical intentions in a score, regardless of the opera's date.

STAGING

the 30-second opera

Staging for the earliest operas

was ostentatious, as rival courts tried to outdo one another in displays of wealth and power. Although budgets tended to diminish when opera became a commercial venture, visual display remained important: designers experimented with scenic perspective and used sophisticated machinery to create special effects. For opera's first three centuries, sets tended to be broadly realistic, until the gradual introduction of more abstract, minimalist stagings (initially for Wagner's operas) from the 1890s. In the later twentieth century, staging practices diversified further and the role of the director became more significant. Now that the operatic repertory is mostly fixed, innovative production styles that update operas and relocate their settings offer a means of creating novelty and maintaining audience interest. *Regietheater*, a term used in continental Europe, denotes productions that depart radically from the prescribed setting, often shifting the action to the present in order to explicitly highlight contemporary politics. References to sex and drugs and the depiction on stage of gratuitous violence have made some such productions highly controversial. Film directors from Franco Zeffirelli to Woody Allen have also tried their hand at opera directing.

RELATED TOPICS
See also
OPERA HOUSE
page 20

GRAND OPÉRA
page 78

3-SECOND BIOGRAPHIES
GIACOMO TORELLI
1608–78
Italian stage designer and an early pioneer of spectacular scenic effects

ADOLPHE APPIA
1862–1928
Swiss architect and stage designer, who designed the first abstract sets for Wagner's operas

PETER SELLARS
1957–
American theatre director, known for controversial updated opera productions

30-SECOND TEXT
Alexandra Wilson

Spectacle and excess were a particular speciality of nineteenth-century French grand opéra.

3-SECOND MOTIF
Staging is a broad term that encompasses not only an opera's sets, but also its costumes, choreography and acting, and the director's 'concept' of a production.

3-MINUTE ARIA
Dramatic conventions have changed in opera over the centuries, with complex codes of symbolic gestures gradually giving way to greater naturalism in acting. The fact that operas are now regularly filmed for DVD or cinema release has considerably altered audience expectations. There is growing pressure for singers to look the part and to act convincingly: the 'park and bark' style of opera where performers simply stand and sing is now less acceptable.

WORDS & MUSIC

cabaletta The cabaletta is the fast, final section of the classic nineteenth-century aria. The mood of the preceding cantabile would be broken in a linking passage called a 'tempo di mezzo' ('middle movement') in which, typically, a messenger would bring in a game-changing piece of news, or the character singing would make a resolution to take some action. The fast and often flashy cabaletta would then be an expression of that resolution or change of mood. Prime examples include one from Verdi's *Il trovatore*, Act 3: the troubadour Manrico, having sung of his love for Leonora in the cantabile 'Ah si ben mio', is alerted to the fact that his mother is to be burned at the stake (*tempo di mezzo*). He resolves to save her – as soon as he's sung his bravura cabaletta 'Di quella pira', replete with several top Cs.

canon A word originally taken from a religious context, the term canon in opera – and the arts in general – refers to a selection of works that have become 'canonized' as acknowledged masterpieces deserving pride of place in the operatic museum. This idea of great masterworks of the past did not take hold until the nineteenth century; works before then had been composed for the moment; as the 1800s progressed, however, composers were increasingly aware of the past and produced their own works with an awareness of posterity. The term has become contested in recent terms and criticized for reflecting the patriarchal, euro-centric (and often Germano-centric) attitudes of the nineteenth century.

cantabile In the classic early nineteenth-century Italian scheme, the cantabile (sometimes also called 'cavatina') would be the main first section of an aria. Slow and reflective in character, the cantabile was usually preceded by a section of scene-setting recitative.

concertato A staple of Italian opera in the nineteenth century, the concertato (short for 'pezzo concertato', meaning literally 'concerted piece') was a moment, usually in a long finale of an act, when the drama would freeze after a dramatic event (often a revelation or a shocking transgression) to give way to a large-scale ensemble, built up layer upon layer, with soloists and chorus gradually joining in. A famous example is 'Di sprezzo degno' which follows Alfredo's public humiliation of Violetta in Act 2 scene 2 of *La traviata*.

intermedio/intermezzo Usually believed to be the main precursor to opera itself, the 'intermedio' was a form of lavish entertainment including music, singing and dancing and devised to fit between the acts of a play performed at court. The earliest records of intermedii date from the late fifteenth century. The related term intermezzo refers to a similar practice that saw discrete comic interludes performed during *opere serie* right up until the Baroque period. The term would make a comeback in the later 1800s, with orchestral intermezzi appearing in late nineteenth-century works such as Puccini's *Manon Lescaut*, *Cavalleria rusticana* (whose intermezzo was made famous by Martin Scorsese's *Raging Bull*) and *Pagliacci*.

motif A term for a musical idea – usually just a few notes, but also possibly running to a few bars – that might be heard several times throughout a work. This idea might also be assigned an 'extra-musical' tag, and in the case of Wagner's leitmotif (literally 'leading motif') technique several might be woven together to suggest further meaning in an orchestral accompaniment.

prelude In instrumental music, a 'prelude', sometimes full of improvisatory flourishes, would often serve as a curtain raiser to another piece or group of pieces, but in the nineteenth century it shed this literal function, with composers producing preludes that stood by themselves and revelled in the freedom offered by the genre. In operatic terms, the prelude was related to the overture, but could ignore the residual conventions sometimes required of the latter. In the later part of the nineteenth century the term 'prelude' was applied to orchestral introductions – often to each act of an opera rather than, as with an overture, only at the very start – that were sometimes relatively brief, more freely descriptive and which often led seamlessly into the action.

symphony/sinfonia The most prestigious instrumental form of Austro-German instrumental music during the nineteenth century, the symphony has its origins in the fast-slow-fast scheme of the Italian opera overture (called a *sinfonia*). With the addition of a further central movement, in the second half of the eighteenth century, the standard scheme of the symphony became established. The most influential examples were by Beethoven, who built on the legacy of his teacher and the 'father of the symphony', Joseph Haydn, as well as Mozart. There was a breakthrough, though, when Beethoven's Ninth and last symphony employed singers and a chorus in its famous finale, something which, Wagner argued, demonstrated the need for a new sort of opera employing the same musical techniques used by the greatest writers of symphonies.

THE OVERTURE
the 30-second opera

The function of the overture is in part explained by its French derivation: *ouverture* means simply 'opening'. Today it might loosely, if inaccurately, be applied to any piece of orchestral music that precedes the action of an opera, but 'overture' as a blanket term only really came into being in the 1800s. The original *ouverture* was a product of the French Baroque, and several Italian equivalents fulfilled a similar role; later developing into the *sinfonia*, these Italian overtures had a fast-slow-fast layout and were a precursor to the symphony. In the eighteenth century, and beyond, some overtures remained generic and non-specific, enabling interchangeability between operas. Others, including Mozart's for *Don Giovanni* and *Così fan tutte*, captured the character of the work in question and even featured music that would appear in the opera. In the nineteenth century, a standard form, particularly in Italian and French opera, became the so-called *pot-pourri* overture, which was essentially a medley of the opera's greatest hits. Others, notably by German composers, would be like expansive symphonic movements. Wagner's *Tristan* and Verdi's *La traviata* are two operas to feature preludes (which can introduce individual acts rather than the whole opera) instead of an overture; other operas, such as Strauss's *Salome*, do away with any sort of introduction at all.

3-SECOND MOTIF
From the very earliest operas, the orchestra has been called upon to bring the audience to attention and set the scene before the action begins.

3-MINUTE ARIA
Many of the great operatic overtures have taken on lives of their own in the concert hall, with some of Beethoven's four overtures for his opera *Fidelio* being prime examples. Another famous overture, Verdi's for *La forza del destino*, was written to replace what in the first version of the opera was a much shorter prelude.

RELATED TOPICS
See also
ORCHESTRA
page 26

WOLFGANG AMADEUS MOZART
page 96

GIUSEPPE VERDI
page 100

RICHARD WAGNER
page 102

30-SECOND TEXT
Hugo Shirley

The blanket term 'overture' covers a range of introductory pieces: some short and self-contained, some a parade of hit tunes, others more ambitious and symphonic.

THE ARIA

the 30-second opera

Arias are the high-points of opera, often literally, where star singers get to show why they are paid so much. Like gladiators, they perform draining physical feats and are immediately rewarded or condemned; even in these days of generally well behaved-audiences, both cheers and boos can still stop the show after a particularly remarkable performance of, say, Verdi's 'Sempre libera' (for soprano, from *La traviata*) or Puccini's 'Nessun dorma' (tenor, *Turandot*). Accordingly, giving individual singers appropriate music (i.e. suited not only to their voice but also to their place in the company pecking order) was always a central fact of life for composers. For librettists, at least until the twentieth century, this meant constructing dramas mainly out of alternations between leisurely moments of stand-and-sing vocal reflection, in which time is as if frozen while a principal character expresses his or her feelings, and rather more frenetic passages containing everything else (explanation, dialogue, reports of events off-stage, physical interaction). As dramatic fashions have changed over the last 150 years or so, this imbalance has been righted. Plot development has become more a part of the stage action, and singers have been obliged to make their mark more succinctly – or at least less repetitively.

RELATED TOPICS
See also
THE RECITATIVE
page 40

GIUSEPPE VERDI
page 100

GIACOMO PUCCINI
page 108

MARIA CALLAS
page 110

3-SECOND BIOGRAPHY
LUCIANO PAVAROTTI
1935–2007
Italian tenor and humanitarian

30-SECOND TEXT
Cormac Newark

Italian tenor Luciano Pavarotti became synonymous with Puccini's aria 'Nessun dorma' after it was used as the theme tune for the 1990 football World Cup in Italy.

3-SECOND MOTIF
For some, the aria is an anti-dramatic moment of singerly indulgence; for others, an oasis of vocal beauty among the incomprehensible shifting sands of operatic plot.

3-MINUTE ARIA
The eighteenth-century aria was very often in *da capo* form – a long 'A' section followed by a shorter, contrasting 'B' section and a repeat, usually decorated with vocal ornaments, of 'A'. In the nineteenth-century Italian tradition, the main sections of a standard aria were the cantabile (slow) and the cabaletta (fast) sections. All such formulas were restrictive, but good composers could manipulate them to produce more dynamic forms. The best among them also knew when to let well alone.

THE RECITATIVE

the 30-second opera

Opera began with recitative: a kind of speech so heightened as to have become music. This is what certain late-seventeenth-century theorists apparently believed to have been standard performing practice in Greek tragedy, and it is to this important-sounding precedent that various operatic reformers have appealed over the intervening centuries. But even the earliest works in the medium contained more self-consciously song-like passages too, and by the end of the seventeenth century the alternation between recitative and aria (or ensemble) was firmly established. The operatic canon, indeed, is mainly made up of eighteenth- and nineteenth-century works that are predicated on it: put crudely, on the difference between singing that is supposed to represent ordinary speech (whether conversational or declamatory) and singing that conveys more poetic thoughts. The latter was more obviously melodic, but some later nineteenth-century composers, notably Wagner, dispensed with the small-scale periodic structures implied by that term. (Wagner called his melodies 'unending'; his critics grumbled that they never began.) This development continued into the 1900s: even allowing for different definitions of melody, most would agree that Debussy's *Pelléas et Mélisande* contains little more than subdued, delicate recitative.

3-SECOND MOTIF
The boring bits between the arias, recitative was before c. 1700–1850 – and arguably since – what entire operas were made of.

3-MINUTE ARIA
In Baroque and Classical opera, and for some of the nineteenth century, *recitativo* could be *secco* (literally 'dry', supported by only a bass line and chords, typically cello and harpsichord) or *accompagnato* ('accompanied', usually by the orchestral string section), with the former being the norm in comic opera and the latter reserved for more intense or otherwise dramatically significant moments.

RELATED TOPICS
See also
THE ARIA
page 38

OPERA SERIA
page 72

OPERA BUFFA
page 74

RICHARD WAGNER
page 102

3-SECOND BIOGRAPHY
CLAUDE DEBUSSY
1862–1918
French composer of the celebrated *Pelléas et Mélisande* (1902)

30-SECOND TEXT
Cormac Newark

The hard-working speech-like element of opera, recitative can be used to set the scene or drive the plot along.

THE CHORUS

the 30-second opera

Inspired by the choruses in

ancient Greek drama, the operatic chorus fulfils the function of commenting on the events unfolding onstage. Choruses also create local colour and a chorus is often used to open an opera as a vivid, immediate way of establishing a work's setting. In early opera, 'choruses' were often sung by the assembled principals but the chorus as a distinct group separate from the soloists yet integral to the action emerged over time. The real heyday of the opera chorus began in the early nineteenth century: as composers wrote increasingly political operas, the chorus came to symbolize the 'voice of the people'. In Italy, many chorus numbers of this period were akin to patriotic hymns, while in spectacle-driven French *grand opéra* the chorus was used for extravagant ceremonial scenes. Opera choruses represent diverse communities (sometimes assuming different guises within a single work), whether soldiers, gypsies, huntsmen, slaves or pilgrims, and have occasionally been used to embody non-human phenomena, such as the storm in Verdi's *Rigoletto*. Certain types of chorus became a stock in trade: every Italian composer from Spontini to Puccini wrote a choral prayer scene. Choruses may console or may terrify, the latter tendency being exemplified by the baying mob in Britten's *Peter Grimes*.

3-SECOND MOTIF
In opera, the term chorus is used both to denote a group of massed singers and the musical numbers that this group sings.

3-MINUTE ARIA
Composers wrote increasingly sophisticated music for choruses as the nineteenth century progressed, although they were sometimes frustrated by chorus members' lack of technical ability and discipline. Chorus members were often ordinary people simply recruited off the streets and were sometimes badly behaved and prone to striking. It was only later in the nineteenth century that permanent opera house choruses started to be established and were given proper training.

RELATED TOPICS
See also
STARS
page 22

ORCHESTRA
page 26

ENSEMBLE
page 46

GIUSEPPE VERDI
page 100

GIACOMO PUCCINI
page 108

3-SECOND BIOGRAPHY
GASPARE SPONTINI
1774–1851
Italian opera composer and conductor

30-SECOND TEXT
Alexandra Wilson

The 'voice of the people', the chorus can be called upon to provide many of opera's most stirring moments.

1820
Born out of wedlock in Stockholm, and spends her childhood unhappily fostered

1838
Makes her debut in Stockholm as Agathe in Weber's *Der Freischütz*

1841
After experiencing vocal problems, goes to study in Paris with Manuel Garcia, who transforms her technique and restores her confidence

1847
Makes a sensational debut in London, where she subsequently creates the role of Amalia in Verdi's *I Masnadieri* and earns the fervent admiration of Queen Victoria and Prince Albert

1849
Makes her final stage appearance as Alice in Meyerbeer's *Robert le Diable*, one of her most famous roles

1850
Embarks on a gruelling concert tour of the USA, organized by P. T. Barnum

1852
Marries composer and pianist Otto Goldschmidt, with whom she has three children. Settling in England, she sings in occasional concerts, but otherwise devotes herself to family life and teaching at the Royal College of Music

1887
Dies at her home in the Malvern Hills

JENNY LIND

Jenny Lind, widely known as the Swedish Nightingale, has some claim to rank as the most famous singer of the Victorian era.

At a time when women performing in opera were widely thought to be little better than courtesans – usually Catholic and Italian to boot – Lind presented herself as the unassailably demure and virginal embodiment of austere Nordic Protestant integrity. Her insistence on her moral respectability makes her sound rather sanctimonious – 'I possess neither the personal advantages, the assurance or the charlatanism of other prime donne' she primly proclaimed – but such statements appealed to a society that made a virtue of hypocrisy. And in her case, there was an unhappy family background and a strangely complicated love life to be concealed.

Her operatic career was relatively brief, focused on a small number of roles and almost entirely confined to Sweden, Germany and England. The lighter demands of winsome Amina in *La Sonnambula* (Bellini) and dainty Marie in Donizetti's *La Fille du régiment* appear to have shown her to her best advantage; she lacked the temperamental authority for more dramatic roles such as Norma and Donna Anna (*Don Giovanni*).

Today we would probably consider her stage personality insipid (and even in her day, racier types found her excessively 'spoony'), but the effortless breath control, tonal sweetness and exquisite pianissimo which marked her flawless technique evidently gave her singing a distinctive magic of its own – Chopin described it 'as a kind of Northern Lights', while Wagner noted her 'curious pensive individuality' and others remarked on her 'woodland freshness' and 'seraphic purity'.

London went wild for her when she made her debut in 1847, and among other things, a tulip, a pub and a whistling kettle were named after her. But the pressures and irritations of performing in the limelight frightened and exhausted her, and as she teetered on the verge of a nervous breakdown after over-work and two unhappy romantic experiences, she announced her retirement from the stage at the age of only 29.

She was, however, unable to resist a stupendous financial offer from the irrepressible showman and impresario P. T. Barnum, who signed her up for an 18-month concert tour of the United States. Lind's appearance in America was heralded by a sophisticated marketing, advertising and PR strategy that reaped enormous ticket sales and profits as well as stimulating a public interest in opera stars which survives to this day.

Rupert Christiansen

ENSEMBLE
the 30-second opera

3-SECOND MOTIF
An important weapon in opera's expressive armoury, ensembles can range from the intimacy of a duet between lovers to the spectacular grandeur of a set piece for full chorus and soloists.

3-MINUTE ARIA
Ensembles often demonstrate a composer's ingenuity, with different voices and dramatic situations weaving together simultaneously (in the intricate *Rigoletto* quartet, for example). On other occasions they raise interesting questions: in the famous quartet of Beethoven's *Fidelio*, for example, four characters express completely different emotions while singing the same melody.

The old saying 'Two's company, three's a crowd' applies to opera too: the most common sort of ensemble is the lovers' duet; a trio often spells trouble. Although not unusual in early opera, numbers featuring more than one character became rare in the convention-bound world of the Baroque. It was primarily in *opera buffa* that ensembles later became a regular fixture: servants and tricksters of comic opera bickered and plotted; aristocrats expressed higher emotions more serenely, and often alone. The extended finale, in which confusion would reign among multiple characters, flourished in comic opera, too: Mozart-Da Ponte operas offer the finest examples, which were inventively followed by Rossini. In more serious operas of the nineteenth century, ensembles had a key role, bringing variety to the musical texture, while grand 'concertato' finales, continued to play a part in Italian opera until the end of Verdi's career. Such formal ensembles largely fell foul of the need for heightened dramatic realism, but duets thrived, with Wagner literally taking them to new lengths in *Tristan und Isolde*. The special power of the clock-stopping set-piece ensemble nevertheless remained, famous examples being the quintet in Wagner's *Meistersinger von Nürnberg* and the trio in Strauss's *Der Rosenkavalier*.

RELATED TOPICS
See also
BEL CANTO
page 76

GRAND OPÉRA
page 78

WOLFGANG AMADEUS MOZART
page 96

GIUSEPPE VERDI
page 100

30-SECOND TEXT
Hugo Shirley

Although operatic ensembles might have characters singing in harmony, they often convey several conflicting emotions.

HISTORY

arioso Derived from the word aria, arioso describes the fluid middle ground between aria and recitative, vocal writing that has the moments of lyrical expansiveness of an aria but is not constrained by the associated conventions. It is a good description of the vocal writing in early opera, as well as of that found in much opera composed today.

CNN opera An expression coined to describe operas, in the late twentieth century and beyond, that took recent news events as their subjects, particularly those events that an audience would themselves have first learnt about through rolling television news channels. See also **Zeitoper**.

intermedio/intermezzo Usually believed to be the main precursor to opera itself, the 'intermedio' was a form of lavish entertainment including music, singing and dancing and devised to fit between the acts of a play performed at court. The earliest records of intermedii date from the late fifteenth century. The related term intermezzo refers to a similar practice that saw discrete comic interludes performed during *opere serie* right up until the Baroque period. The term would make a comeback in the later 1800s, with orchestral intermezzi appearing in late nineteenth-century works such as Puccini's

Manon Lescaut, *Cavalleria rusticana* (whose intermezzo was made famous by Martin Scorsese's *Raging Bull*) and *Pagliacci*.

historically informed performance (HIP) Also referred to as authentic or period-instrument performance, this movement, reaching its heyday in the 1980s, sought to re-create the original conditions of musical performance, stripping away what were believed to be 'inauthentic' practices accumulated over the centuries. This has helped the rediscovery of many works in Early and Baroque opera in particular, and sometimes even extends to trying to re-create productions from the period. A lack of documentary evidence – and the impossibility of such evidence adequately describing historical practices – means, however, that many such performances are speculative; critics have argued that they actually reflect more about our own time than the time they seek to recapture.

leitmotif The term, meaning 'leading motif', coined to describe a technique pioneered by Wagner and brought to fruition in his vast cycle of four operas *Der Ring des Nibelungen*. It built on earlier devices of the 'reminiscence motif', whereby certain characters and ideas would be associated with a musical idea that reappeared throughout a work. Wagner's great innovation was threefold, however.

There would be a far greater number of these motifs and they would often be manipulated (as Berlioz had manipulated the *idées fixes* or 'fixed ideas' of his orchestral music) and woven into one another. The result was a musical language that could be understood to take on something approaching specific meaning. The term itself was not coined by Wagner.

pasticcio A form of operatic hotchpotch, most common in the Baroque period, where arias, choruses and ensembles from several different existing works would be brought together in the service of a new plot. The full-scale *pasticcio* fell out of fashion in the eighteenth century, as operatic composers reacted more specifically to the dramatic situation in hand. Elements of the practice persisted in Italian opera into the nineteenth century, with 'suitcase arias', substitutions and reworkings, often necessitated by straightforwardly pragmatic reasons. There have been occasional *pasticcios* in recent times, too, with the Metropolitan Opera's *The Enchanted Island* the most high-profile example.

repertory The word has two meanings in operatic context. First, it refers simply to those works that are regularly performed around the world, and which have established themselves as part of the regular repertoire. One might also, however, refer to an opera house with a 'repertory system', where a large number of works would rotate in the active repertoire. The other main system is the 'stagione' (Italian for 'season') system, where a smaller number of works will be performed in more concentrated periods.

suitcase aria A term used to describe arias that opera stars would bring with them wherever they went to sing: they would be packed, the phrase suggests, along with everything else in their luggage. These arias, often of usefully generic style or content, would be interpolated into whichever opera the singers had been engaged to perform in.

Zeitoper In some ways an earlier manifestation of the 'CNN opera', the *Zeitoper* (from German, meaning literally 'time opera' or 'opera of the time') would be work that sought specifically to capture something contemporary, rather than dealing with the mythical or historical subjects that had so often been the standard. Not unrelated to the earlier Italian school of verismo, *Zeitoper* reflected a desire in Weimer-era Germany to create art that reflected rather than amplified real life.

BEGINNINGS

the 30-second opera

In sixteenth-century Italy,

theatrical spectacle, instrumental dance music, solo song and the madrigal were fused together in the *intermedio*: a lavish court entertainment designed to accompany a play. The difference between this and opera was simple but radical: in opera, the drama would be sung in music that imitated the rhythms of speech (recitative) over a simple bass line, with harmonies improvised on the lute, keyboard, harp or viol, and the stories, drawn from Classical mythology, were told in a different way. In Monteverdi's *L'Orfeo* (1607), we hear the earliest surviving example of music being used to define character, mood and place. Opening out from the recitative, arioso sections find a voice weaving in counterpoint to bass lines drawn from established instrumental forms. The art of virtuosic decoration, both instrumental and vocal, was highly prized. From the cadences of different languages, national styles developed. In Venice's public theatres, Cavalli built on Monteverdi's legacy in works such as *Il Giasone* (1649). Steffani took Venetian opera north to Munich in the 1670s, while in France Italian-born Lully established a native form with his *tragédies lyriques*. The reign of Charles II, raised in exile in France, would see two of the earliest English operas: Blow's *Venus and Adonis* (1683) and Purcell's *Dido and Aeneas* (1689).

3-SECOND MOTIF
With speech as its model, the new art form advanced rapidly to incorporate vocal and instrumental music of great sophistication, often combining high tragedy and low comedy.

3-MINUTE ARIA
From the courts of Mantua and Florence, opera spread to the public theatres of Venice and Naples, and across the Alps. An Italian-born composer established a French national style, rich with dance music and exotic instrumental effects, that would go on to influence the first English operas.

RELATED TOPICS
See also
THE ARIA
page 38

THE RECITATIVE
page 40

CLAUDIO MONTEVERDI
page 92

3-SECOND BIOGRAPHIES
FRANCESCO CAVALLI
1602–76
Italian composer of popular, often bawdy or satirical Venetian operas

JEAN-BAPTISTE LULLY
1632–87
Italian-born composer, a Louis XIV favourite and creator of a national operatic style in France

HENRY PURCELL
1659–95
English composer of masques, semi-operas and opera influenced by Lully and pre-Restoration English theatre music

30-SECOND TEXT
Anna Picard

Early opera is often wildly imaginative and irreverent, and speaks powerfully today.

BAROQUE
c. 1650–1750

the 30-second opera

The Venetian model in which

serious drama and carnival bawdiness co-existed was slowly replaced by two distinct forms, *opera seria* and *opera buffa*, the latter pioneered in Naples from the 1660s and infused with the folk music and dialect of that region. The division between recitative and aria was gradually formalized, the aria becoming an extended platform for a character's expression of elation, fury or despair. The cult of the star-singer began, with some artists commanding extraordinary fees and demanding music that flaunted their technical agility and expressive power. In early eighteenth-century England *opera seria* gained great popularity as Handel and his rivals vied to seduce the audience with stories of kings and queens before London succumbed to the demotic charms of the ballad opera, typified by Gay's *Beggar's Opera* (1728). In Vienna, Vivaldi enjoyed brief success but suffered an impoverished death. The pasticcio proliferated, a drama with music drawn from several composers. In Germany, Telemann wrote polyglot operas, with some arias sung in German, some in Italian. Charpentier refined the *tragédie lyrique* in *Medée* (1693), but Rameau revolutionized French opera with *Hippolyte et Aricie* (1733) and the scorching dissonance of the 'Trio des Parques'. Ballet, integral since the reign of Louis XIV, remained central to the style.

3-SECOND MOTIF
The Baroque era saw the birth of the star-singer and the showcase aria, the reign of the castrato, and the development of distinct serious and comic genres.

3-MINUTE ARIA
The arrival of so-called historically informed or authentic performance in the final decades of the twentieth century brought with it an increased interest in long-forgotten corners of the Baroque repertoire, finding new strategies to make its sometimes formal language speak to audiences today.

RELATED TOPICS
See also
THE ARIA
page 38

THE RECITATIVE
page 40

OPERA SERIA
page 72

OPERA BUFFA
page 74

3-SECOND BIOGRAPHIES
ANTONIO VIVALDI
1678–1741
Italian composer more famous in his lifetime for his more than 40 operas than for his instrumental music

JEAN-PHILIPPE RAMEAU
1683–1764
French theorist and composer whose innovative use of harmony scandalized and charmed the Paris audience

30-SECOND TEXT
Anna Picard

The Baroque period saw opera become both increasingly formalized and extravagantly fantastical.

CLASSICAL
c. 1750–1800

the 30-second opera

3-SECOND MOTIF
Melodic elegance and clear textures characterize the Classical period, and even such a complex form as opera was able to shed some of its grandeur.

3-MINUTE ARIA
The year 1762 was one of the great turning points in operatic history: nothing could be the same after the premiere of Gluck's *Orfeo ed Euridice*, which launched the composer's manifesto for reform of opera. His high-minded aim of achieving dramatic truth was to leave its mark even on the great opera composers of the next century.

Having established itself so comprehensively in the first half of the 1700s, *opera seria*'s influence lingered well into the Classical period. Two of Mozart's mature operas were to embrace the form, and he was one of several composers in the late eighteenth century still to be setting the texts of arch-librettist Metastasio. But Mozart's achievements would have been impossible without Gluck, who, caught up in a great Parisian debate about operatic aesthetics, set out to dispense with the Baroque excesses of 'Italian' opera and aim at 'beautiful simplicity'. This reaches a highpoint in the lofty restraint of Gluck's *Iphigénie en Tauride* but would have been unthinkable without the musico-dramatic earthquake of his own, earlier *Orfeo ed Euridice*, a familiar operatic subject set in his new, unextravagant style. Yet the era was not all about seriousness, and Mozart again set standards in *opera buffa*, especially in collaboration with Da Ponte. Next to the towering figures of Gluck and Mozart, other operatic composers are easily overlooked, but J. C. Bach, Salieri, Haydn and Grétry feature, discarding Baroque's conventions for a clearer, more flexible musical language. Alone at the end of this succession, straddling the Enlightenment and Romanticism, is Beethoven, whose one opera, *Fidelio*, mixes conventional with revolutionary, operatic with symphonic.

RELATED TOPICS
See also
OPERA SERIA
page 72

OPERA BUFFA
page 74

3-SECOND BIOGRAPHIES
PIETRO METASTASIO
1698–1782
Italian poet considered the most important opera seria librettist

LORENZO DA PONTE
1749–1838
Venetian poet and librettist

CHRISTOPH WILLIBALD GLUCK
1714–1787
German composer of French and Italian opera who served as operatic father figure to Mozart

30-SECOND TEXT
John Allison

The Classical period saw the stripping away of much excess in opera, with Gluck, in particular, seeking to underline dramatic truth.

ROMANTIC
c. 1800–1850

the 30-second opera

RELATED TOPICS
See also
BEL CANTO
page 76

GRAND OPÉRA
page 78

GIOACHINO ROSSINI
page 98

3-SECOND BIOGRAPHIES
JOHANN WOLFGANG
VON GOETHE
1749–1832
German poet and playwright

WALTER SCOTT
1771–1832
Scottish novelist, poet and
playwright

CARL MARIA VON WEBER
1786–1826
German composer, conductor
and critic prominent in the
Romantic period

3-SECOND MOTIF
Everything in opera started to grow in the Romantic period: the voices, the size of the orchestra, theatres and audiences, not to mention the emotions.

3-MINUTE ARIA
Despite – or perhaps because – musical Romanticism trailed historically behind its literary counterpart, the great Romantic writers left a deep mark on opera. Authors such as Goethe, Pushkin and Scott, whose idealized, windswept and heather-strewn version of Scotland appealed to the Italians in particular, were set more widely than almost anyone since Shakespeare.

National styles competed to define the operatic landscape during much of the nineteenth century. Beethoven's influence was wider than his single opera (*Fidelio*) legacy would suggest, most obviously among German composers. Weber, who was well-placed to build on the folkish nationalism of the Romantic movement, revelled in natural and supernatural worlds and cultivating a richly orchestral operatic language. Wagner explored similar themes in his early operas on medieval and supernatural subjects, while being increasingly concerned with questions of German national identity. Beethoven also inspired Berlioz, one of the leading figures in France alongside Meyerbeer, whose *grands opéras* came to define several decades of Parisian style from the 1830s. Rossini, among the most orchestrally minded of early nineteenth-century Italian composers, was another admirer of Beethoven, but began by writing the comedies on which his reputation largely still rests. His immediate successors, Donizetti and Bellini, refined the *bel canto* style, building on Rossini's ambitious later works to prepare the way for Verdi, who never looked back after the nationalistic success of his third opera, *Nabucco*. The rise of nationalistic opera across many oppressed or ill-defined nations reflected the increased political turmoil across Europe by mid-century, with historical or folkish subjects – lovers often providing a powerful combination.

30-SECOND TEXT
John Allison

As opera became increasingly engaged with politics, it began more and more to be inspired by folklore and history.

LATE NINETEENTH CENTURY

the 30-second opera

The mature works of Wagner

and Verdi stand as the major achievements of late nineteenth-century opera, yet they continue to dominate our picture of this period because of the influence they exerted on the operas of emerging composers. Strauss and Puccini, their direct musical descendants, made their most lasting operatic mark after 1900, though the latter's *La Bohème* (1896) reflects a new spirit of freshness found in many operas of the time. In Italy, the 1890s witnessed the rise of the verismo movement, and something similar had already been developing in France at least since the premiere in 1875 of Bizet's *Carmen*. Many other French composers, including Gounod, Saint-Saëns, Massenet and (the German-born) Offenbach, built on their country's long operatic tradition, so what really distinguished the late nineteenth century was the emergence far away from opera's old power bases – Italy, Germany, France – of new national schools. This had already been seen some decades earlier in the work of such composers as Glinka (Russian), Moniuszko (Polish), Smetana (Czech) and Erkel (Hungarian); in the masterpieces of Dvořák, Mussorgsky, Rimsky-Korsakov and even the more western-looking Tchaikovsky, we see how opera houses became a focal point for the national aspirations arising throughout Europe.

RELATED TOPICS
See also
VERISMO
page 86

GIUSEPPE VERDI
page 100

3-SECOND MOTIF
As the nineteenth century progressed, opera became increasingly of the people, reflecting a drift away from the loftier operatic subjects of earlier times.

3-MINUTE ARIA
While the history of opera in the second half of the nineteenth century was in some ways a story of two grand traditions – the French and the Italian, embodied by Verdi – coming up against the newly prominent school of German opera (embodied by Wagner and those who propped up his legacy after his death), it is also a story of increased turning away from those, with opera expressing and exploring nationalist feelings and traditions in self-consciously nationalist ways.

3-SECOND BIOGRAPHIES
MIKHAIL GLINKA
1804–57
Russian composer

FERENC ERKEL
1810–93
Hungarian composer, the father of Hungarian grand opera

MODEST PETROVICH MUSSORGSKY
1839–81
Russian composer and innovator of Russian music during the Romantic period

30-SECOND TEXT
John Allison

Operas telling stories based in everyday life, such as La Boheme *were an emerging trend in the late nineteenth century.*

LA

HENRY MURGER

BOHÈME

CARMEN

Opéra-Comique en quatre actes

1873
Born in poverty in Naples and sings as a child in church choirs

1895
Makes his professional operatic debut in Naples

1902
Makes his first recording and his debut at Covent Garden, singing in *Rigoletto* opposite Nellie Melba

1903
After five years of sensational success in Italy, makes his debut at the Metropolitan Opera, where he will give over 800 performances

1906
Embarrassed after being convicted (perhaps wrongfully) of molesting a lady in the monkey house of the zoo in Central Park

1910
Creates role of Dick Johnson at the Metropolitan in Puccini's *La Fanciulla del West*

1921
Dies in Naples from pulmonary illness, exacerbated by heavy smoking

ENRICO CARUSO

There is something marvellously straightforward and communicative about Caruso's art, as many of his 250 surviving recordings bear witness. There seems to be no protective film of mechanical technique or self-conscious artifice cast over the glowingly warm and resonant sound he makes: nothing preciously operatic or intellectually calculated taints it. Here is someone, we feel, who opened his mouth and his throat and sang from the engine of his natural God-given musicality.

The man himself was spiritual twin to the singer. 'His humanity was deep, his humour was broad, his faith was high,' wrote his wife Dorothy, and even if prim and rigid souls occasionally found his flirtatious twinkle and penchant for pranks alarming, he was loved and revered wherever he went – and his travelling through Europe and the Americas during his two decades of superstardom was incessant and ultimately exhausting.

As a performer, he was immediate, instinctive and openly emotional, which is one reason that his interpretations of Puccini and the verismo composers still sound so modern and vivid. His version of the aria 'Vesti la giubba' from *Pagliacci*, in which Canio laments his wife's adultery, was the first disc ever to sell over a million copies, and however familiar it has become, the intensity of its grief still scalds. And has anyone made 'E lucevan le stelle', Cavaradossi's farewell to life and love in *Tosca*, so meltingly poignant, or Rodolfo's courting of Mimi in *La Bohème* more shyly ardent?

Caruso did not sing Wagner or Mozart, but his range was nonetheless broad. He could declaim the arias of *Aida* and *Samson et Dalila* with powerful nobility, he could sparkle through the bucolic comedy of *L'Elisir d'Amore* or relax in the simple melodies of humble songs from his beloved native Naples. He was without snobbery, musical or otherwise: he always sang generously.

Caruso had only sporadic vocal training when he was young, and much ink has been vainly spilt attempting to analyse and unlock the method behind his magic. Imitating him remains impossible, but thanks to the rich recorded legacy, his achievement has been so inspirational to the likes of Beniamino Gigli, Mario Lanza, Jussi Bjorling, Luciano Pavarotti, Placido Domingo, Roberto Alagna and Joseph Calleja that a century after his death, he remains the living fount of the great tradition of Italianate tenors.

Rupert Christiansen

TWENTIETH CENTURY

the 30-second opera

Some predicted the demise of opera after Puccini's death: the posthumous premiere of his *Turandot* in 1926 certainly signalled the end of an era. However, although increasingly facing the challenge of the silver screen for the public's attention, opera had extraordinary operatic vitality in the first half of the last century, with the premieres of all the major stage works of such composers as Richard Strauss and Janáček. Above all Debussy's *Pelléas et Mélisande* (1901) expressed the musical world as it stood at the start of the century, strongly influencing what followed, despite such major modern voices as Berg, Stravinsky, Bartók, Shostakovich, Prokofiev, Hindemith, Weill and Martinu having their very individual say. A postwar thread initiated increased experimentation both in the way new operas were composed and old ones staged, although the most avant-garde modernist works of this time have struggled to remain in the repertory. Probably the most defining trend of the century has been the rise of opera in English on both sides of the Atlantic – reflected in the work of Britten, Tippett, Birtwistle, Glass, Reich and Adams. Indeed, the emergence of so-called 'CNN opera' (exemplified in Adams's *Nixon in China*) was hardly surprising, and confirms that opera remains keen to address political issues.

3-SECOND MOTIF
In a turbulent century, one that saw the rise of cinema as a new form of popular entertainment, nothing changed so radically as the way in which opera was consumed.

3-MINUTE ARIA
The recording industry took off in opera at the start of the century with Caruso, who was also to participate in the first live radio broadcast (1910) from New York's Metropolitan Opera. The constant march of improving technology, giving audiences ownership of audio and visual recordings of repertoire works and even ultra-rare pieces, made it easier to enjoy opera at home.

RELATED TOPICS
See also
ENRICO CARUSO
page 62

LEOS JANÁČEK
page 114

BENJAMIN BRITTEN
page 116

3-SECOND BIOGRAPHIES
MICHAEL TIPPETT
1905–98
English composer

HARRISON BIRTWISTLE
1934–
English composer

JOHN ADAMS
1947–
American composer

30-SECOND TEXT
John Allison

From **Pelléas et Mélisande** *to* **Nixon in China,** *opera in the twentieth century proved to be a vibrant and endlessly resilient art form.*

TWENTY-FIRST CENTURY

the 30-second opera

Although our technology-driven age means that audiences can experience a performance – or a form of it – even on a hand-held digital device, fundamental components of opera have changed surprisingly little. One of the most successful operas of the twenty-first century to date premiered right at its start: Saariaho's *L'Amour de loin* (2000) which, while typical of the composer's musical modernism, is based on a twelfth-century tale. Old subject-matter prevails as much as ever; our new century still awaits the emergence of a radically fresh operatic aesthetic. Many of the major works so far are by composers who established their styles before 2000; many have also mined their subjects from such traditional sources as Greek myth (Birtwistle's *Minotaur*), Shakespeare (Adès's *Tempest*) and various literary classics. Others – Adams, Glanert and Glass – have been building on their past outputs. Works addressing our time or the future have been rare, though a major exception is Ruders's *The Handmaid's Tale*, drawn from Margaret Atwood's dystopian novel of the same name. Smaller-scale works return opera to its roots and may well prove more practical and financially viable, a factor to consider as opera continues to compete in an increasingly crowded world of arts and entertainment.

3-SECOND MOTIF
Having adapted to 400 years of changing historical, social, economic and political conditions, opera remains resilient, while new technologies – such as web streaming and the HD cinecast – have perhaps made it more accessible than ever.

3-MINUTE ARIA
The Zeitoper label, usually applied to 'operas of the time' from Weimar Germany, describes works that paraded technologies and attitudes of the period. Few twenty-first-century operas have fully embraced modern developments, but those that have include Nico Muhly's cyber-thriller *Two Boys*, exploring the world of internet chat rooms and online relationships, and Tod Machover's *Death and the Powers*, using robots, live electronics and digital participation by the audience.

RELATED TOPICS
See also
OPERA HOUSE
page 20

JOYCE DIDONATO
page 146

3-SECOND BIOGRAPHIES
POUL RUDERS
1949–
Danish composer

KAIJA SAARIAHO
1952–
Finnish composer

30-SECOND TEXT
John Allison

Opera has held its own into the twenty-first century, taking advantage of the technological developments to be able to reach wider audiences worldwide.

GENRES

aria di bravura An aria – invariably fast, usually carefully positioned within an opera to achieve maximum effect – designed specifically to show off a singer's technical attributes. Such devices employed might be florid runs or coloratura, high notes (with the option for the performer to add in plenty of his or her own). The arias themselves were often written with a particular singer (and their attributes and skills) in mind.

aria di sortita see exit aria

chest voice This term means two different things, referring to the top of the male voice and the lower reaches of a female voice – when each is delivered at full throttle. In the case of male singers (and tenors in particular) the high-wire, chest-voice top notes that are so synonymous with the voice today were an innovation of the second quarter of the nineteenth century. Until then such notes would have been sung in 'head voice' or *voix mixte*, a cultivated half-falsetto sound which still remains in the modern singer's expressive vocabulary. The chest voice in female singers refers to something close to the more natural speaking voice, which is pushed into service to bolster lower notes often to powerfully dramatic, if sometimes unrefined, effect.

exit aria Translation of '*aria di sortita*' (Italian). The exit in 'exit aria', somewhat counterintuitively perhaps, refers not to exiting *from* the stage but *onto* the stage at the end of a carefully plotted scene. In the strictly formal world of eighteenth-century *opera seria*, then, an exit aria would be the first aria – usually attention-grabbing and offering details pertinent to the exposition of the plot in question – that each main character would sing.

falsetto The method of singing in which only the edges of the vocal chords vibrate, by which, in particular, male artists are able to sing in the soprano and alto ranges, as most often employed these days by countertenors and male altos (although some operas require lower male voices to sing falsetto for comic effect – Marcello in Act 4 of *La Bohème* for example, or Falstaff in Act 1 of Verdi's eponymous opera).

operetta Originating in Paris in the 1850s, operetta (meaning, literally, 'little opera', and in earlier times also applied straightforwardly to smaller-scale operatic works) was established as a satirical and genuinely comic alternative to the increasingly non-comic and pretentious *opéra-comique*. The works of Jacques Offenbach, setting the pattern of quick-fire dialogue interspersed with musical numbers, in particular, relentlessly poke fun at established operatic traditions, as well as all elements of the wider establishment, a tradition taken up by Gilbert and Sullivan in Britain. Viennese operetta, which reached its heyday around the turn of the twentieth century, provides a characteristic mix of humour and nostalgia while also reflecting political concerns – a mixture that can often be seen in the twentieth-century musical, a closely related genre.

Singspiel Growing out of German-language traditions mixing music and words, the Singspiel was, until the nineteenth century, the dominant model for 'German' opera. The name combines two German words – 'sing', as in English, and 'spiel', meaning play – and the genre reflects that relatively straightforward duality, with discrete musical numbers (often more reflective than dramatic) breaking up the action of a play. Official attempts were made on occasion in German-speaking lands to position *Singspiel* as a valid alternative to the Italian opera preferred by the upper classes (one result was Mozart's *Die Entführung aus dem Serail* of 1781), yet it perhaps remained most vibrant as a popular genre, as reflected in the often pantomime-like *Die Zauberflöte* (Mozart's singspiel of 1791).

Sprechgesang Literally meaning 'speech-song', Sprechgesang is a German word denoting a form of notated, half-sung speech that was employed by composers in the twentieth century. Famous operatic examples can be found in Arnold Schoenberg's *Moses und Aron*, where Moses's Sprechgesang reflects the character's own philosophical and dramatic predicament, and Alban Berg's two operas *Wozzeck* and *Lulu*.

symphony/sinfonia The most prestigious instrumental form of Austro-German instrumental music during the nineteenth century, the symphony has its origins in the fast-slow-fast scheme of the Italian opera overture (called a *sinfonia*). With the addition of a further central movement, in the second half of the eighteenth century, the standard scheme of the symphony became established. The most influential examples were by Beethoven, who built on the legacy of his teacher and the 'father of the symphony', Joseph Haydn, as well as Mozart. There was a breakthrough, though, when Beethoven's Ninth and last symphony employed singers and a chorus in its famous finale, something which, Wagner argued, demonstrated the need for a new sort of opera employing the same musical techniques used by the greatest writers of symphonies.

OPERA SERIA
the 30-second opera

As it emerged in the early 1700s,
Italian *opera seria* (literally, 'serious') was a genre of music drama governed by Aristotelian precepts and Enlightenment good taste. Librettos were organized in short scenes dominated by the concluding 'exit' aria, in which whatever advance in the plot had occurred in the recitative would be summed up and reflected upon. Duets and trios among the principals were possible but much less frequent, and arias usually fell into one of a relatively small number of categories. Notable among these was the *aria di bravura*, a virtuosic display-piece that became especially identified with the castrati. These were the on-stage stars of *opera seria*, feted all over Europe, but the off-stage maestro was the highly influential librettist Metastasio, whose texts dominated the genre. He so perfected its conventions that it was easy for parts of one work to be transplanted into another, with top singers regularly substituting their own favourite or newly composed arias for the originals. *Opera seria*, popular until the beginning of the nineteenth century (Haydn wrote at least three), fell out of fashion until its comparatively recent revival (above all the examples by Handel, mainly written for London 1720–37) by the early music movement.

3-SECOND MOTIF
Some examples of *opera seria* feature over 30 arias, others have solos that last a quarter of an hour each: that's serious opera in any language.

3-MINUTE ARIA
Opera seria, originally the product of a late-seventeenth-century reform that sought to raise the tone of operatic subjects to the aesthetic heights of French neo-classical theatre, was itself repeatedly reformed. Various librettists and composers (including Jomelli, Traetta and Gluck, the latter most famously in his *Orfeo* of 1762) varied the structure and content of their works in an effort to make them more dramatically compelling and less dependent on celebrated soloists.

RELATED TOPICS
See also
THE ARIA
page 38

THE RECITATIVE
page 40

BAROQUE
page 54

GEORG FRIDERIC HANDEL
page 94

3-SECOND BIOGRAPHIES
PIETRO METASTASIO [TRAPASSI]
1698–1782
Italian poet and librettist

CHRISTOPH WILLIBALD GLUCK
1714–87
German composer

JOSEPH HAYDN
1732–1809
Austrian composer

30-SECOND TEXT
Cormac Newark

Highly formalized and often unrealistic, Opera Seria has brought out the best in many great composers.

OPERA BUFFA

the 30-second opera

Opera buffa was born at the beginning of the eighteenth century in Naples. Like *opera seria*, its slightly older and better-behaved sister, it comprised a substantial *sinfonia* (overture), three acts, and an alternation of recitative and (mainly) *da capo* arias. It also involved a certain amount of vocal gender confusion, but, unlike *opera seria*, the confusion resulted from cross-dressing rather than castration. Also, in early examples, the arias are not showy or indeed even very difficult, having been intended for actors rather than professionally trained singers. The genre spread throughout Italy, reaching Venice by the late 1840s, where it found its first ideal composer-librettist combination in Galuppi and (the already-famous playwright) Goldoni. It then became popular all over Europe, and a second dream-team emerged a few decades later in Vienna: Da Ponte and Mozart, whose *Le nozze di Figaro*, *Don Giovanni* and *Così fan tutte* (1786–90) represent the pinnacle of the genre in scale, complexity and (occasionally) seriousness. But it was Rossini, working with no matter which librettist or format (his comic operas are in two acts or, in the case of the early farces, one), who was crowned undisputed king of the buffo style with such masterpieces as *L'Italiana in Algeri* (1813) and *Il barbiere di Siviglia* (1816).

RELATED TOPICS
See also
OPERA SERIA
page 72

WOLFGANG AMADEUS MOZART
page 96

GIOACHINO ROSSINI
page 98

3-SECOND BIOGRAPHIES
BALDASSARE GALUPPI
1706–85
Italian composer

CARLO GOLDONI
1707–93
Italian playwright and librettist

LORENZO DA PONTE
1749–1838
Italian librettist

30-SECOND TEXT
Cormac Newark

With plots usually set in everyday life and with non-aristocratic, comic protagonists, opera buffa depends on deliberately far-fetched scenarios.

3-SECOND MOTIF
It really is funny: unlike French *opéra comique*, which often isn't even intended to amuse, Italian *opera buffa* still makes audiences laugh all over the world.

3-MINUTE ARIA
The earliest works in the genre were in Neapolitan dialect, and some later examples combined Italian (for the principals) and Neapolitan (for the secondary, more consistently comic characters). Throughout the later history of the genre, the words of *opera buffa* have tended to lend themselves much more readily to translation into the local language than the more self-consciously poetic librettos of tragic works.

BEL CANTO

the 30-second opera

The Italian phrase *bel canto*

means, quite simply, beautiful singing. In operatic history, though, its sense is a little more complex: it has usually been used to describe an aesthetic, a method or a sound that has, regretfully, been lost. This recurring idea that opera used to be so much better than it is now doubtless says something important about the conservative tendencies of its audiences more broadly (or possibly just their advanced age), but vocal technique did change quite markedly over the course of the nineteenth century. Since then, the term has been particularly associated with the voices that Rossini, Donizetti and Bellini had in mind when composing their operas, voices trained in the glorious tradition of the *castrati*: even and highly flexible across the whole range, capable of executing intricate ornamentation (often improvised), and generally lighter in tone than those that succeeded them. A *bel canto* 'revival' in the middle of the twentieth century heralded the return to the repertory of many works of Donizetti and Bellini especially, as well as the worldwide celebrity of certain specialized performers, notably the sopranos Beverly Sills and, perhaps above all, Joan Sutherland.

RELATED TOPICS
See also
GIOACHINO ROSSINI
page 98

GIUSEPPE VERDI
page 100

3-SECOND BIOGRAPHIES
GIOVANNI BATTISTA RUBINI
1794–1854
Italian tenor

GAETANO DONIZETTI
1797–1848
Italian composer

VINCENZO BELLINI
1801–1835
Italian composer

30-SECOND TEXT
Cormac Newark

3-SECOND MOTIF
The old joke *bel canto* = 'can belt-o' is quite wrong: the style pre-dated the vocal trials of strength introduced by Verdi, Wagner and Puccini.

3-MINUTE ARIA
Perhaps the clearest differences between *bel canto* singing and later styles are to be heard in the principal tenor roles of Italian operas premiered in the 1820s and 30s, some written specially for the legendary Rubini. The high parts of this music, originally composed to be performed using a kind of expressive falsetto, are extremely challenging for today's singers, who are trained to sing everything with the chest voice.

Australian soprano Joan Sutherland was instrumental in reigniting interest in bel canto in the twentieth century .

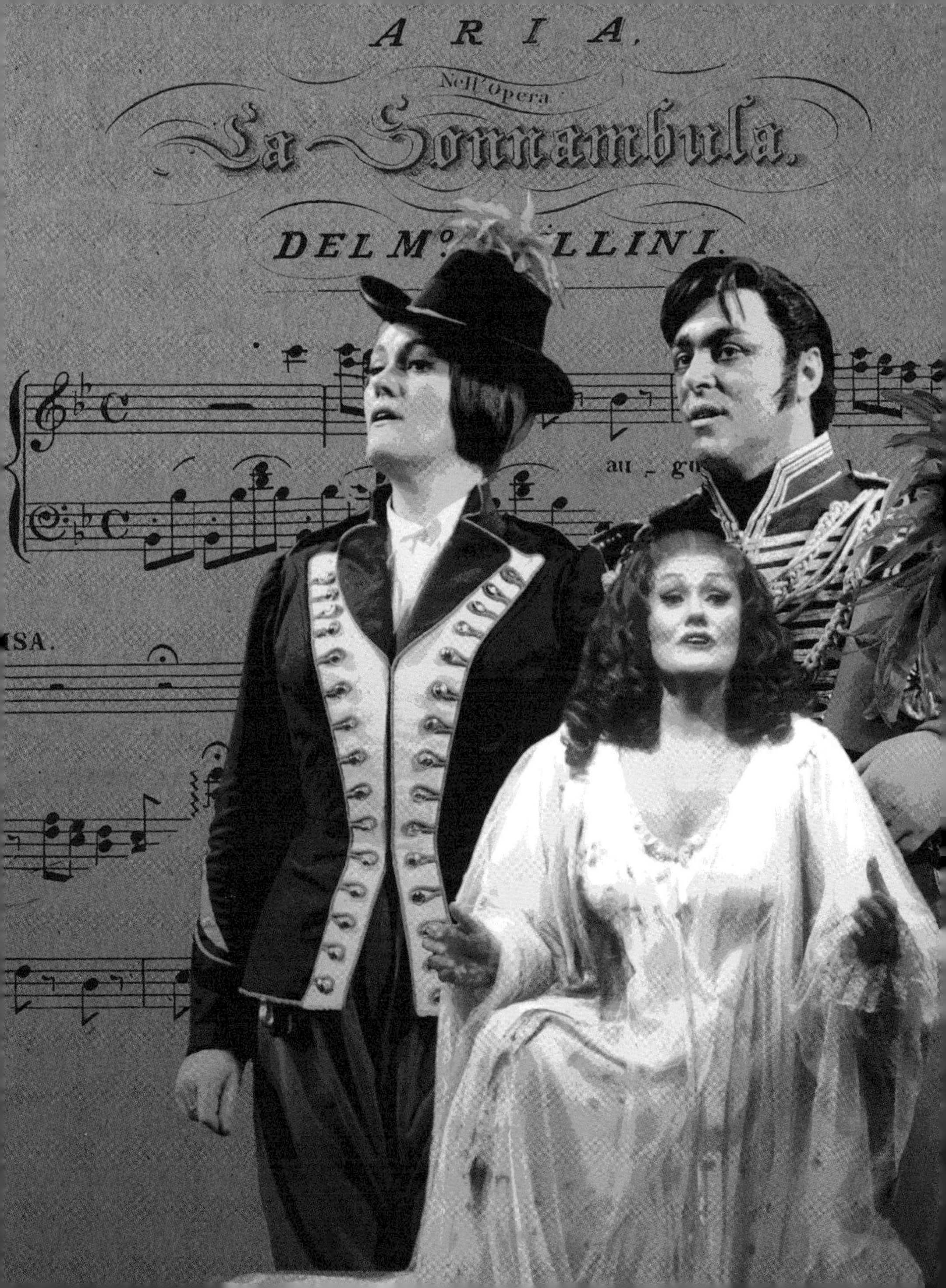
ARIA,
Nell' Opera
La Sonnambula.
DEL Mo. LLINI.
au - gu
ISA.

GRAND OPÉRA
the 30-second opera

These days, especially in the US, 'grand opera' usually means any tragic opera sung throughout (that is, without any spoken dialogue). *Grand opéra*, on the other hand, refers to a genre that became popular in Paris in the late 1820s, declined over the 1850s and welcomed its last major new works to the stage in the 1860s, but in the meantime was exported all over Europe and beyond. It was characterized by an emphasis on spectacle, with the extravagant costumes and effects for which opera had always had a weakness enhanced by a new, much more complex kind of staging and some legendary *coups de théâtre* (erupting volcanoes, exploding castles, shipwrecks, that sort of thing). There was also an obligatory ballet episode, a large chorus and extras in their hundreds. Last, and sometimes even more expensive, *grand opéra* demanded more principal singers than other genres. These played characters who were not exclusively noble, as was the case in serious opera up until then, and this contributed to another defining feature: the plots almost always included large-scale social conflict. Most of the composers who were successful in the genre are no longer well known, but Rossini and Verdi contributed important examples.

RELATED TOPICS
See also
THE CHORUS
page 42

ROMANTIC
page 58

GIOACHINO ROSSINI
page 98

GIUSEPPE VERDI
page 100

3-SECOND BIOGRAPHIES
DANIEL AUBER
1782–1871
French composer

GIACOMO MEYERBEER
1791–1864
German composer who trained in Italy and settled in France

FROMENTAL HALÉVY
1799–1862
French composer

30-SECOND TEXT
Cormac Newark

Before cinema, the spectacular tableaux characteristic of grand opéra offered flamboyant and exciting entertainment.

3-SECOND MOTIF
The dinosaur of operatic genres: enormous, dominating, roamed the entire world for ages, died out suddenly and completely, now endlessly fascinating to historians.

3-MINUTE ARIA
For most of the nineteenth century, opera production in Paris was strictly divided between institutions; *grand opéra* was the special preserve of the most important, the Paris Opéra (from 1875, based at the Palais Garnier), and remained in the repertory there more or less until the First World War. It was arguably the Opéra's close identification with the French state itself, and the resulting insistence on magnificence, that gave *grand opéra* its distinctive character.

1873
Born in Kazan, the son of peasants, and sings in the Russian provinces before studying in Tbilisi

1901
Begins his international career at La Scala, singing in Boito's *Mefistofele*

1910
Creates the title role in Massenet's *Don Quichotte*

1894
Joins the Imperial Opera (Mariinsky Theatre) in St Petersburg, moving to Moscow two years later

1908
Begins appearances in Paris and London under the auspices of Diaghilev's Russian seasons

1921
Leaves Russia on tour, never to return

1937
Gives final stage performance, at the Monte-Carlo Opera

1938
Dies of leukaemia in Paris and is laid to rest there until 1984, when his tomb was moved to Moscow's Novodevichy Cemetery

FYODOR CHALIAPIN

Few artists have had their autobiographies ghosted by major literary figures, but then Fyodor Chaliapin was as big a star in the Russian cultural firmament as any of its writers. In the words of Maxim Gorky, who produced Chaliapin's memoirs, 'In Russian art, Chaliapin, like Pushkin, is an epoch'. Even such an outwardly severe figure as Tolstoy was seen furtively wiping away tears when he heard Chaliapin sing, afterwards sending him his complete works inscribed with a dedication. An immense and magnetic presence on the stage – a bear of a man, Chaliapin stood well over six feet tall – he exercised a huge fascination over everyone who heard him, and even over those who had merely heard of him.

Chaliapin was most famous of all for his portrayal of Mussorgsky's Boris Godunov, the tormented tsar whose death scene is one of the peaks of operatic literature. His costume for Boris's coronation scene (he was a perfectionist who looked after his own costuming and make-up) was heavy enough to require two people to lift it. None of his great successors in this part – such basses as Boris Christoff, Nicolai Ghiaurov, Nicola Ghiuselev, Yevgeny Nesterenko – is ever believed to have equalled the vocal and dramatic power of Chaliapin's assumption.

His name is almost as inseparable from such roles as Rossini's Don Basilio, Verdi's King Philip, Boito's *Mefistofele* (after hearing Chaliapin's interpretation, the composer exclaimed, 'At last I have found my devil!') and Massenet's Don Quichotte, a part composed especially for him. He also created the role of the jealous Salieri in Rimsky-Korsakov's Pushkin-derived *Mozart and Salieri*. Typical of his artistry was his ability to sing three roles in Borodin's *Prince Igor* (Igor, Galitsky and Konchak).

Reports of Chaliapin's live performances and even old recordings testify to the extraordinary magnitude of his bass voice, deep and rich with tangible vibrations; he left several versions of Mussorgsky's 'Song of the Flea', each like an operatic scene in miniature. But in life he wore something of a theatrical mask too, few getting close to the man who was mistrustful of most around him. A master not only of opera but also the dramatic stage, he was the first reformer of twentieth-century opera: as the great director Konstantin Stanislavsky admitted, 'My system is taken straight from Chaliapin.'

John Allison

OPERA WITH DIALOGUE

the 30-second opera

From the mid-1900s, most German comic opera (known as *Singspiel*) used passages of spoken dialogue, often containing farcical banter: Mozart's *Die Zauberflöte* for example. Operas with more serious plots – Beethoven's *Fidelio* and Weber's *Der Freischütz* – adopted this custom in the Romantic era, until Wagner's insistence that music was capable of expressing everything made it seem passé. But in the last century, modernist composers such as Schönberg and Berg developed a technique of loosely pitched, rhythmic speech – *Sprechgesang* (speech-song), a distant precursor of rap or hiphop. A strain of French opera called *opéra-comique* but not necessarily comic, also used spoken text: original versions of Bizet's *Carmen* and Gounod's *Faust* involved dialogue, although this was later replaced by musical recitative. Operetta is partially defined by its inclusion of spoken scenes: works by Lehár, Offenbach, Gilbert & Sullivan and J. Strauss are rich in dialogue, as are their descendants the classic American musical comedies by Rodgers and Sondheim. A few operas otherwise entirely set to music occasionally use brief episodes of speech to heighten dramatic effect: powerful examples are Violetta's reading of Germont's letter in the final scene of Verdi's *La Traviata* and the climax of Britten's *Peter Grimes*, where Grimes is told to scuttle his boat.

3-SECOND MOTIF
Spoken text plays an important part in several operatic traditions, used to advance the plot and provide contrast with the musical numbers.

3-MINUTE ARIA
Most opera resolves the unstable relationship between what is sung and what is said by means of a divide between the purely melodic aria and the connecting 'recitative', in which the singing voice becomes conversational. But sometimes ordinary speech is used too.

RELATED TOPICS
See also
THE RECITATIVE
page 40

ROMANTIC
page 58

3-SECOND BIOGRAPHIES
JACQUES OFFENBACH
1819–80
German-born master of Parisian operetta, whose compositions include the famous can-can, from his irreverent reworking of the Orpheus myth, *Orphée aux Enfers*

W.S. GILBERT
& ARTHUR SULLIVAN
1836–1911 & 1842–1900
English librettist and composer who created 14 comic operas, many premiered in London's Savoy Theatre

30-SECOND TEXT
Rupert Christiansen

Composers from Verdi to Berg and Britten have used spoken passages to special dramatic effect in their operas.

MUSIC DRAMA

the 30-second opera

In the fraught business of operatic classification 'music drama' is one of the most slippery of genres. It is most closely associated with Wagner, who avoided the term but theorized at length about the need to reposition drama, as opposed to music, as the main concern of the operatic stage. This was to be serious opera, set up against the supposed frivolity of the dominant French and Italian composers who – according to the egomaniacal Wagner – pandered to the whims of egomaniacal singers. Ironically, of course, the earliest operas in Italy were designated *Dramma per musica*, but the formalization of some sorts of opera in later centuries had arguably seen music become the tail that wagged the dramatic dog. As the nineteenth century progressed, this balance redressed, not only with Wagner but also with the later works of Verdi. Other significant composers whose operatic works might be called music dramas include Mussorgsky, the raw power of whose music matched the craggy political subjects he chose to set. A further irony, and one that arose not least in Wagner's works, was that in abandoning the formal schemes of arias and set pieces, the music in 'music dramas' became increasingly symphonic, with acts composed as vast, overarching paragraphs and governed by new musical conventions.

RELATED TOPICS

See also
LIBRETTO
page 16

ORCHESTRA
page 26

LATE NINETEENTH CENTURY
page 60

RICHARD WAGNER
page 102

30-SECOND TEXT
Hugo Shirley

3-SECOND MOTIF
The idea of 'music drama' articulates a renewed engagement in the nineteenth century with the familiar operatic debate between words and notes, singing and acting, stage and pit – in short, between music and drama.

3-MINUTE ARIA
Relatively few works are actually designated 'music drama' as a genre, but the term might be loosely applied to any operatic piece in which traditional numbers give way to 'through-composed' music that runs continuously without breaks, and in which more 'naturalistic' dramatic rhythm is unimpeded by formal musical conventions.

Wagner's **Ring** *cycle set out to place drama centre stage, with music there to serve it.*

Oper und Drama

Von Richard Wagner.

VERISMO

the 30-second opera

Verismo is a specifically Italian

brand of operatic realism, which flourished between 1890 and the 1910s and developed out of the sort of psychological realism explored in Verdi's mid to late operas. There was a slightly earlier literary Verismo movement, and composers based their operas on the short stories of writers such as Giovanni Verga. Verismo operas are often set in the impoverished and 'exotic' Italian south (usually Naples or Sicily) and deal with gritty, sordid situations: typical characters are prostitutes, criminals or peasants. The genre is passionate and highly charged but the emphasis is more on sensationalism than sentimentalism and love is presented in its most raw, lustful forms. This type of opera tends to limit its dramatic focus to a single situation or event and use it to explore the themes of jealousy, betrayal and revenge. Typically fast paced, Verismo hurtles towards its dénouement (usually a crime of passion), with no scope for complicated subplots or back-stories. Many Verismo composers wrote one-act works, the ideal format for creating a broad-brush 'slice of life'. It is customary to find two Verismo operas paired as a double bill, most regularly Mascagni's *Cavalleria rusticana* and Leoncavallo's *Pagliacci*. Puccini is often mistakenly labelled a 'Verismo' composer: his only work in this style is *Il tabarro*.

RELATED TOPICS
See also
ROMANTIC
page 58

TWENTIETH CENTURY
page 64

GIUSEPPE VERDI
page 100

GIACOMO PUCCINI
page 108

30-SECOND TEXT
Alexandra Wilson

3-SECOND MOTIF
Verismo is the short, sharp shock of the operatic world: 'man loves wife, wife takes lover, man kills lover' is a typical plot.

3-MINUTE ARIA
Verismo operas are performed in a highly flamboyant manner, combining full-blooded lyricism with desperate sobs, brutal shouts and hysterical laughter. Composers from the Verismo school sometimes quoted from popular culture of the day, inserting guitar- or mandolin-accompanied folksongs and regional dances to provide local colour. The orchestration in a Verismo opera is typically heavy and the orchestra is sometimes spotlighted in an intermezzo.

Although Puccini's **Tosca** *does not fall into the classic Verismo canon, its pace and its plot, which climaxes in a murder/suicide, has similarities with works in the genre.*

KEY COMPOSERS

concerto Similar in form to the Symphony, the concerto would feature a solo instrument (but also, particularly during the Baroque period, more than one) playing with an orchestra. The three-movement solo concerto became the norm in the second half of the eighteenth century, with Mozart's for piano (he wrote 27) often containing aria-like slow movements.

crescendo A term (literally meaning, 'growing') indicating that music should get louder. In a score it might be abbreviated to 'cresc.' or represented graphically by a hairpin (<) stretched out to indicate the length of the crescendo. 'Decrescendo' (or 'decresc.') is the opposite, represented by a hairpin pointing the other way (>).

intermedio/intermezzo Usually believed to be the main precursor to opera itself, the 'intermedio' was a form of lavish entertainment including music, singing and dancing and devised to fit between the acts of a play performed at court. The earliest records of intermedi date from the late fifteenth century. The related term intermezzo refers to a similar practice that saw discrete comic interludes performed during *opere serie* right up until the Baroque period. The term would make a comeback in the later 1800s, with

orchestral intermezzi appearing in late nineteenth-century works such as Puccini's *Manon Lescaut*, *Cavalleria rusticana* (whose intermezzo was made famous by Martin Scorsese's *Raging Bull*) and *Pagliacci*.

madrigal A form of vocal composition dating back to the late thirteenth century, the madrigal was usually composed for several voices to secular texts, meaning that it could develop complexities that would not have been permitted in sacred music. Monteverdi's madrigals are perhaps the finest, and while the form originated in Italy, it was imported to many other European countries, including to Elizabethan England.

'The Mighty Handful' (sometimes called 'The Five') This group of Russian composers (Mussorgsky, Rimsky-Korsakov, Borodin and the now less well-known Balakirev and Cui) set out to build a Russian operatic tradition on the foundations laid by Glinka and his operas (including *Ruslan and Ludmilla* and *A Life for the Tsar*). Largely self-taught, these five had an ambivalent relationship towards Tchaikovsky, whose music was deemed to be too 'western'. More broadly, the group reflected the nationalism that spread across many countries outside the traditional operatic centres of Europe (France, Germany and Italy).

operetta Originating in Paris in the 1850s, operetta (meaning, literally, 'little opera', and in earlier times also applied straightforwardly to smaller-scale operatic works) was established as a satirical and genuinely comic alternative to the increasingly non-comic and pretentious *opéra-comique*. The works of Jacques Offenbach, setting the pattern of quick-fire dialogue interspersed with musical numbers, in particular, relentlessly poke fun at established operatic traditions, as well as all elements of the wider establishment, a tradition taken up by Gilbert and Sullivan in Britain. Viennese operetta, which reached its heyday around the turn of the twentieth century, provides a characteristic mix of humour and nostalgia while also reflecting political concerns – a mixture that can often be seen in the twentieth-century musical, a closely related genre.

oratorio A sacred cousin to opera, the oratorio is typically a composition that sets a sacred text adapted, usually, from the Bible for a number of soloists, chorus and orchestra. Sometimes the oratorios, although rooted in the concert hall, can come close to opera in their dramatic power, and several in the early eighteenth century were, essentially, operas in sacred garb. Handel's oratorios are among the best known and the most operatic: several, including *The Messiah* and *Saul*, have been staged by opera companies.

polyphony A term that can refer, in basic terms, to music consisting of several parts moving with a certain independence – polyphonic as opposed to monophonic. More broadly, though, polyphony might refer to an early vocal music tradition, dating back to the eleventh century, that arguably found its highpoint in the sixteenth century, in the sacred music of such composers as Lassus, Victoria, Byrd and Palestrina.

through-composed A term applied to operas where whole acts and scenes are 'composed through', meaning there is less sense of the individual, discrete arias, ensembles and choruses that were the norm in operas from the Baroque period through to the second half of the nineteenth century. The ultimate 'through-composed' operas are the mature works of Wagner, and Verdi's late operas *Otello* and *Falstaff* as well as the works of Puccini would show their influence in breaking down the distinction between distinct numbers.

CLAUDIO MONTEVERDI 1567–1643

the 30-second opera

Monteverdi's *L'Orfeo* (1607) is the earliest surviving opera to describe character and situation in music. The role of the demi-god who descends to Hades to reclaim his dead wife, charming the gods with his song 'Possente spirto', was written for virtuoso tenor Francesco Rasi, the instrumental music, built on a thick bed of lutes, harp and regal organ, for specific players at the court of Mantua. *L'Orfeo* presaged the deaths of Monteverdi's wife, Claudia, and his pupil Caterina Martinelli. All that remains of his next opera, *Arianna*, is the lament, 'Lasciatemi morire'. Many compositions were lost. What survives from Monteverdi's old age are two operas written for the public theatres of Venice that define the city's sardonic humour: *Il ritorno d'Ulisse in patria sua* (1640) and *L'incoronazione di Poppea* (1643). Both open with prologues in which the gods present the argument; both contrast the machinations of the ruling class with the low humour of their servants, including the stock travesty role of the aged nurse, sung by a tenor. In Penelope, who remains faithful to Ulysses, and Poppea, who displaces Ottavia in the affections of the murderous Nero, Monteverdi created two magnetic female characters. Seneca occupies a stygian soundworld last heard in *L'Orfeo*, while Ottavia's lament 'Addio Roma' is a startling expression of bitterness and loss.

RELATED TOPICS
See also
ORCHESTRA
page 26

THE ARIA
page 38

THE RECITATIVE
page 40

BEGINNINGS
page 52

3-SECOND BIOGRAPHIES
JACOPO PERI
1561–1633
Italian composer of the first opera, *Dafne* (1598)

FRANCESCO RASI
1574–1621
Italian tenor and lutenist who created the role of Orfeo

GIACOMO BADOARO
1602–54
Venetian librettist of *Il ritorno d'Ulisse in patria sua*

30-SECOND TEXT
Anna Picard

Monteverdi is believed to have written 18 operas, but only two survive in their complete form.

3-SECOND MOTIF
Monteverdi took elements of the Renaissance intermedio and extended and blended them into something new, finding compelling ambiguities in characters from antiquity and Classical mythology.

3-MINUTE ARIA
All three of Monteverdi's surviving operas are notable for their bold instrumental and stylistic contrasts, with dynamic dance music, extended laments, duets of great sensuality and madrigalian ensembles. Modern audiences have struggled with the moral bleakness of *Poppea*, in which two unpleasant characters seemingly triumph. Monteverdi's original audience would have known that their reign would end in grotesque violence.

VLISSE

GEORG FRIDERIC HANDEL 1685–1759

the 30-second opera

RELATED TOPICS
See also
THE ARIA
page 38

THE RECITATIVE
page 40

BAROQUE
page 54

OPERA SERIA
page 72

3-SECOND MOTIF
Tremendous imagination within the apparently rigid musical and dramatic conventions of *opera seria* and the *da capo* form; Handel's operas are remarkable for their emotional sophistication and humanity.

3-MINUTE ARIA
Though Handel's choral music remained popular throughout the centuries after his death, his operas were forgotten until the 1920 revival of *Rodelinda*. Buoyed by research into historical performance practice, interest in his operas gathered pace in the 1980s. Works such as *Rinaldo* and *Partenope* moved into mainstream repertoire, and as rarities such as *Poro* and *Giustino* are revived, recent years have seen persuasive stagings of his sacred oratorios *Theodora*, *Jephtha* and *Susanna*.

Born in Germany and later

adopted by the English, Handel found his voice in Italy, creating a catalogue of melodic and harmonic ideas that would continue to evolve in his later work. *Agrippina*, premiered in Venice, is notable for the unapologetic immorality of its characters, the scintillating diversity of the instrumental writing and the sensuality of the duet 'No, no ch'io non apprezzo'. Though celebrated for the brilliance of his arias, Handel's duets contain some of his most affecting music. He settled in England in 1711 and the main characteristics of his London operas are typical of the era: a grand orchestral overture with dynamic dotted rhythms; a plot that is propelled by recitative and concludes with a *coro* (chorus). Tyrants are vanquished, lovers reunited, thrones restored. What distinguishes Handel's London works is his appetite for innovation and the psychological acuity of his writing. He revitalized the 'mad scene' in *Alcina* and *Orlando* and responded imaginatively to individual artists, whether castratos, tenors or sopranos. Handel composed some 40 operas or operatic works: *Giulio Cesare, Rodelinda, Xerxes, Tamerlano, Acis and Galatea* and the secular oratorio *Semele* are among those to have become core repertoire.

3-SECOND BIOGRAPHIES
NICOLA HAYM
1678–1729
Italian librettist who worked with Handel on ten operas, including *Giulio Cesare*, *Rodelinda* and *Tamerlano*

SENESINO
1686–1758
Italian castrato, creator of the title roles of *Giulio Cesare* and *Orlando*

30-SECOND TEXT
Anna Picard

Revival in interest in Handel's operas has revealed psychological depths he achieved within the formal constraints of his time.

George Frideric Handel

WOLFGANG AMADEUS MOZART 1756–1791

the 30-second opera

Over his tragically short career,

Mozart earned his enduring place as perhaps the most purely 'sublime' of all composers by writing across all genres, but one of his most outstanding contributions was in opera. Particularly in the Italian comedies he wrote with librettist Da Ponte, he produced works of previously unknown musico-dramatic complexity, notable for sureness of pace. Though *Le nozze di Figaro* and *Don Giovanni* have never lost popularity, *Così fan tutte* – once considered immoral – has come to be recognized as not only the most perfectly balanced but also modern of these operas for its subtle, unsettling exploration of human emotions. Mozart wrote the first of his numerous operas as a teenager, but in the regular operatic repertoire his reputation rests on these and four other, very different masterpieces. The unrelenting intensity of *Idomeneo*, premiered just two days after his 25th birthday, marks it out both as the pinnacle of *opera seria* tradition and a work that breaks the bonds of that strict and serious form, one to which Mozart returned with radical concision at the end of his life with the political drama *La clemenza di Tito*. Equally at home in popular German-language theatre, he wrote with magnificent virtuosity in *Die Entführung aus dem Serial* and mixed spectacle with philosophical depth in *Die Zauberflöte*.

RELATED TOPICS
See also
CLASSICAL
page 56

OPERA SERIA
page 72

OPERA BUFFA
page 74

3-SECOND MOTIF
Die Zauberflöte, dating from the last year of Mozart's life, raises enigmatic questions about how his operatic style might have developed had he lived longer.

3-MINUTE ARIA
Despite his status as prince among all Austro-German composers, Mozart occupies a unique position in balancing northern and southern artistic sensibilities. His background had been rooted in the polyphonic traditions of the north, but his achievements in the realm of Italian opera influenced all his music – extending not least to aria-like slow movements in his piano concertos.

3-SECOND BIOGRAPHY
LORENZO DA PONTE
1749–1838
Italian librettist who wrote the librettos for three of Mozart's Italian comic operas

30-SECOND TEXT
John Allison

Mozart's magpie genius allowed him to draw from a wider range of styles and influences from an early age, but his operatic reputation lies largely on his mature masterpieces.

GIOACHINO ROSSINI
1792–1868

the 30-second opera

Often called 'the swan of

Pesaro', after his hometown, or just 'the immortal Rossini', he was the most famous Italian opera composer – indeed the most famous Italian full stop – between about 1815 and 1853 (when Verdi assumed the mantle). He worked in all the major opera centres of Italy, especially Naples, Rome and Venice, and latterly in Paris. Although now most often celebrated for his comedies, his early *opere serie* (notably *Tancredi*, 1813) and his Parisian *grands opéras* (*Guillaume Tell*, 1829) are extremely important in the history of those genres. More generally, Rossini played a significant role in the development of conventions (for example governing the form of arias and the scene-complexes in which they were placed) that became established in early- and mid-nineteenth-century Italian opera. Perhaps the most characteristic element of the Rossinian aesthetic, though, is the frenetic pace of the musical and stage action (presaged in the 'Rossini crescendo' that is a famous feature of many of his overtures, much enjoyed in concert performances too) and the resulting total bewilderment at a given point in the plot (a hilarious example is the sextet 'Questo è un nodo aviluppato'/'This is a tangled knot' from Act 2 of *La Cenerentola*, 1817).

RELATED TOPICS
See also
OPERA BUFFA
page 74

BEL CANTO
page 76

GRAND OPÉRA
page 78

GIUSEPPE VERDI
page 100

3-SECOND BIOGRAPHIES
MARIE-ANTOINE
(ANTONIN) CARÊME
1784–1833
French chef and friend
of Rossini

MARIA MALIBRAN
1808–36
Paris-born mezzo-soprano
and daughter of tenor Manuel
Garcia, greatly admired by
Rossini, many of whose great
roles she created

30-SECOND TEXT
Cormac Newark

Rossini's operas in a variety of genres assure his standing as the most popular Italian composer of his generation.

3-SECOND MOTIF
Rossini was the most famous, successful and influential operatic composer of his day; his retirement at the height of his powers remains one of the great unsolved mysteries of music history.

3-MINUTE ARIA
Owing to his seeming laziness and superficiality following his retirement aged only 37, not to mention his portly build, Rossini's interest in cuisine assumed disproportionate significance in the popular perception of the composer. Many recipes are named after him, some created by his friend, Parisian chef Antonin Carême (whose surname, ironically given the rich and expensive dishes for which he is famous, is the French word for Lent).

GIUSEPPE VERDI
1813–1901

the 30-second opera

Verdi is in many ways the

quintessential Italian opera composer. Not only did his fame coincide, and become intertwined, with the climax of the struggle for unification, he felt moved to assert, towards the end of his life and in the face of foreign encroachments led by Wagner, what he saw as specifically Italian operatic qualities. He had in mind melody and formal intelligibility; judging by his own works, one might add intense characterization and a taste for melodramatic situations to the list. In fact his style developed considerably over a career spanning over 50 years and at least 27 operas (depending on the number of major revisions one counts), and incorporated features from Donizettian Romantic tragedy and Rossinian *opera buffa* as well as French *opéra comique* (*Un ballo in maschera*) and *grand opéra* (*Les Vêpres siciliennes, Don Carlos*), but was always characterized by a search for theatrical effect and, above all, conciseness. Some of his works became staples of the repertory almost instantly (especially the early 1850s 'trilogy' of *Rigoletto, Il trovatore* and *La traviata*), some comparatively recently (*Don Carlos*). Others belong to a revered 'patriotic' canon (*Nabucco*), but his entire oeuvre is nothing less than central to what is understood by the word opera – not just Italian.

RELATED TOPICS
See also
THE ARIA
page 38

ROMANTIC
page 58

GRAND OPÉRA
page 78

BARITONE/BASS-BARITONE
page 132

3-SECOND BIOGRAPHIES
FRANCESCO MARIA PIAVE
1810–76
Italian librettist

CAMILLE DU LOCLE
1832–1903
French theatre director
and librettist

ARRIGO BOITO
1842–1918
Italian librettist, composer
and poet

30-SECOND TEXT
Cormac Newark

*Verdi's long creative
life saw many changes
in opera — some
instigated by
his own work.*

3-SECOND MOTIF
Verdi is the elder statesman, literally, of Italian opera: world-famous by 40, a member of parliament by 50, he composed his last opera aged 80.

3-MINUTE ARIA
Verdi lived long enough to seem conservative to post-unification generations of Italian composers, but this should not obscure what he added to the tradition they inherited. His legacy included a change in singing style and voice classification (especially the 'Verdi baritone'), a more individual musical characterization (making stock roles a thing of the past) and a much more muscular orchestra (rhythmically incisive and, in his critics' view, noisier).

RICHARD WAGNER 1813–1883

the 30-second opera

RELATED TOPIC
See also
CONDUCTOR
page 28

There is no more debated, loved and hated composer than Wagner. According to one memorably hyperbolic statement only Jesus and Napoleon have more books written about them than Wagner. It's no hyperbole, though, to state that he revolutionized opera: he wrote his own librettos; he discarded the rules of traditional opera and transformed the art form; he built his own opera house in Bayreuth. A revolutionary in early life, he, like many fellow Germans at that time, was anti-Semitic and virulently nationalistic, a fact that, allied with the extraordinary power his works exerted on later generations, has made him uniquely contentious. But Wagner's mature operas display humanity, psychological subtlety and philosophical complexity – usually of a pessimistic, unresolved sort that actively questions the idea of heroism – that belie his image in the popular imagination. Things do not end well, for example, for the sword-brandishing, helmet-clad hero and heroine in the four-opera *Ring des Nibelungen*, which occupied Wagner for 25 years and in which he fully introduced his leitmotif technique. *Tristan und Isolde* broke the rules of harmony to convey an eroticism and passion that was deemed dangerous to civilization; his final opera, *Parsifal*, fuses the religious and the sexual with music of sublime mysteriousness in a heady cocktail that left a generation of artists drunk with admiration.

3-SECOND MOTIF
Opera, music and much else besides would never be the same after Wagner, whose almost superhuman ambition informed every aspect of his life and work.

3-MINUTE ARIA
Wagner saw himself as the inheritor of Beethoven and Shakespeare and set out to draw, as had Greek drama, on myth for his subject matter so as to help define Germany and its people through art. Wagner's operas share many thematic links, mediating on similar subjects: redemptive love v. sexual love, the power of art, human fallibility

3-SECOND BIOGRAPHIES
COSIMA WAGNER
1837–1930
Daughter of Hungarian composer Franz Liszt, who married Wagner in 1870 and presided over Bayreuth after his death

FRIEDRICH NIETZSCHE
1844–1900
German philosopher who worshipped Wagner before their monumental falling out

KING LUDWIG II
1845–86
The 'mad' King of Bavaria who saved Wagner from his debts and funded him through much of his creative life

30-SECOND TEXT
Hugo Shirley

Demanding to perform and still uniquely controversial, Wagner's operas are nonetheless unrivalled in their scope and ambition.

GEORGES BIZET
1838–1875

the 30-second opera

Georges Bizet wrote one of the most widely popular of all operas – *Carmen*. In his short life he began numerous other operatic projects, bringing just a handful of them to completion. He was born in Paris in 1838 to a musical family and by the age of ten was studying at the Paris Conservatoire. Once his education was complete, he repeatedly tried to interest Parisian managements in his projects, though there were few takers. *Carmen* represented an act of faith in him from the management of the Opéra-Comique, though the violent story of an immoral gypsy girl who leads a Spanish soldier astray and ends up being stabbed by him was strong meat for the theatre's regular clientele; the composer's severe disappointment following the indifferent first-night reception on 3 March 1875 was a cause, some said, of his early death three months later, aged 36. Yet within a year the scandalous opera was a hit in Vienna, then Brussels, then everywhere else – though it took eight years for Paris finally to accept it. Since then, its combination of popular Spanish idioms and realistic emotion assembled with classic Gallic grace has proved unbeatable – on stage, on film and in every other conceivable medium.

3-SECOND MOTIF
In Bizet's *Carmen* Spanish popular rhythms provide a colourful background to a tale of naked emotions that has appealed to the widest audiences.

3-MINUTE ARIA
Les Pêcheurs de perles (*The Pearl Fishers*) is the most famous of Bizet's other operas, largely due to its stunning tenor/baritone duet, 'Au fond du temple saint'. *La Jolie Fille de Perth*, based on a novel by Sir Walter Scott (*The Fair Maid of Perth*) contains fine music, including a haunting tenor serenade, but suffers from a cumbersome plot. With its oriental setting and lightweight manner, the one-act *Djamileh* is a masterpiece awaiting its hour.

RELATED TOPICS
See also
TENOR
page 128

BARITONE/BASS-BARITONE
page 132

THE FEMME FATALE
page 142

3-SECOND BIOGRAPHIES
LUDOVIC HALÉVY
1834–1908
French writer, one of the librettists of *Carmen*, nephew of composer Fromental Halévy, he first achieved fame as co-librettist of Offenbach's *Orphée aux enfers*

CHARLES GOUNOD
1819–93
French composer of *Faust* and *Roméo et Juliette*, a friend and mentor of the young Bizet

30-SECOND TEXT
George Hall

A failure at its premiere, Carmen grew quickly in popularity after Bizet's early death and today it is an opera-house staple across the world.

PYOTR ILYICH TCHAIKOVSKY 1840–1893

the 30-second opera

On the list of great composers

for the stage, Tchaikovsky comes first among the Russians. He completed ten operas (alongside three of the world's best-loved ballets), though only a handful of these have a regular place in theatres outside Russia. His three finest operas are all drawn from Pushkin, the first of which, *Eugene Onegin*, remains unique in operatic literature for being not so much an 'opera' (as the composer never called it) as 'lyric scenes', an intimate, anti-operatic work dealing with the real-life emotions of unrequited then thwarted love. Inspired by one of Pushkin's cynical little ghost stories, *The Queen of Spades* also deserves its place in the operatic canon, its rich score inhabiting the same emotional world as Tchaikovsky's late symphonies. Less familiar, *Mazeppa* is closer to the rival territory of the five overtly nationalist composers known as The Mighty Handful, some of whom resented their contemporary's success. Another of Tchaikovsky's own nationalist phase is the comedy *Cherevichki*, demonstrating a more colourful, fantastic style. His cosmopolitan instincts, stemming perhaps from a lifelong idolization of Mozart and setting him apart from other leading Russian composers, are reflected in two French-inspired works, *The Maid of Orleans* and *Iolanta*, the latter his haunting, one-act operatic swansong.

3-SECOND MOTIF
The expressive depth and melodic appeal of Tchaikovsky's music is encapsulated in Tatyana's passionate outpouring in the Letter Scene of *Eugene Onegin*.

3-MINUTE ARIA
Tchaikovsky's status as an operatic composer has perhaps been affected by the popularity of his vast opus of symphonies, concertos, chamber works, songs and other music. But, given that the writing of operas is the most labour-intensive form of composition, it would be no exaggeration to say that Tchaikovsky spent most of his creative life in the preparation of works for the stage.

RELATED TOPICS
See also
LATE NINETEENTH CENTURY
page 60

3-SECOND BIOGRAPHY
ALEKSANDR PUSHKIN
1799–1837
Russian author and poet said to be the founder of modern Russian literature

30-SECOND TEXT
John Allison

A disputed figure in contemporary debates regarding Russian musical nationalism, Tchaikovsky created an acknowledged masterpiece in **Eugene Onegin,** *which manages to be simultaneously realistic and achingly lyrical.*

GIACOMO PUCCINI
1858–1924
the 30-second opera

Puccini was the leading Italian

opera composer of the late nineteenth and early twentieth centuries. *Manon Lescaut* (1893) was his first international hit and the three ensuing works, *La Bohème*, *Tosca* and *Madama Butterfly*, are some of the most frequently performed of all operas. Later he experimented with various genres: operetta (*La rondine*), comedy (*Gianni Schicchi*) and one-act opera (the *Il trittico* trilogy). His works feature humble characters – including students (*La Bohème*), gold-miners (*La fanciulla del West*) and barge workers (*Il tabarro*) – and the plight of ordinary people in tragic circumstances, such as Madama Butterfly, prompts great empathy. He went to considerable lengths to evoke the musical ambience of his locations, whether by recreating the precise pitches of the bells of Rome for *Tosca* or by researching authentic Chinese melodies for *Turandot*. He was held up as a successor to Verdi, yet arguably learnt more from Wagner: Puccini's works are largely through-composed and make sophisticated use of motifs, while the orchestra is key in telling the story. He cultivated a flexible, spontaneous musical language, often conversational in style, befitting his realistic subject matter. Yet all of his works, even the most harmonically adventurous, contain moments of the most radiant, impassioned lyricism that underlies his enduring appeal.

RELATED TOPICS
See also
ROMANTIC
page 58

VERISMO
page 86

GIUSEPPE VERDI
page 100

RICHARD WAGNER
page 102

3-SECOND MOTIF
Passionate music, a vivid sense of theatre and emotional situations with universal appeal: these are the hallmarks of Puccini's operas.

3-MINUTE ARIA
Puccini is the ultimate 'love him or loathe him' opera composer. Ever since his own lifetime, critics have attacked his works for being emotionally 'manipulative' and for dealing with 'the little things in life', but it is precisely these qualities that have endeared his operas to audiences worldwide. Puccini's memorable music has been widely used in popular culture and influenced numerous twentieth-century film music composers.

3-SECOND BIOGRAPHIES
GIULIO RICORDI
1840–1912
Italian editor and music publisher who promoted Puccini's operas

GIUSEPPE GIACOSA
& LUIGI ILLICA
1847–1906 & 1857–1919
Italian librettists who worked with Puccini on his most famous operas

30-SECOND TEXT
Alexandra Wilson

Puccini's operas, tuneful, lively and engaging, have at times suffered critically for their enduring and broad popularity.

1923
Born in New York to
Greek parents

1937
Emigrates to Athens,
where she studies
throughout the war with
the Spanish coloratura
soprano Elvira de Hidalgo

1947
Makes her Italian debut
at the Verona Arena in
the title role of *La
Gioconda*

1950
Makes debut at La Scala,
Milan, where over the
next ten years she is
worshipped – and
sometimes reviled

1959
Begins to neglect her
career after falling in
love with Greek shipping
magnate Aristotle
Onassis and leaving
her husband

1964
Briefly returns to the
stage in triumph, singing
the title role in Zeffirelli's
production of *Tosca* at
Covent Garden

1973
Embarks on an artistically
disastrous 'comeback'
recital tour with the tenor
Giuseppe di Stefano,
making her final public
appearance in Japan
in 1974

1977
Dies suddenly in Paris,
in circumstances that
have never been fully
explained

MARIA CALLAS

The triumph and tragedy of

Maria Callas have become so ingrained in legend that it has become hard to form a fair assessment of her artistic achievement, and even harder to understand what motivated her angry, egocentric personality.

She was always fighting someone – her family, impresarios, colleagues, friends, but perhaps most often herself. A fat, plain and unloved child of unsympathetic parents, she struggled tooth and nail to dig her way out of war-torn Athens and become not only the great international prima donna but also a glamorously svelte figure of café society and the jetset. It was a long journey, and only someone of indomitable willpower could have weathered it.

Throughout the 1950s, she flourished – superb productions were meticulously showcased for her at La Scala, Milan, and she became synonymous with the revival of interest in the so-called bel canto operas (the title roles in Bellini's *Norma* and Donizetti's *Anna Bolena* being among her finest roles). She was a magnificent interpreter of Verdi, Puccini and the Verismo composers too, as much admired for her incandescently powerful acting as she was for the rigour and sensitivity of her vocalizing.

It didn't last long. Technical problems – notably an unpleasant wobble on sustained top notes – which first emerged in the mid-1950s worsened and could not be eliminated, and her personal life disintegrated after she left her dull but shrewd husband for the brutally nasty Aristotle Onassis, who then abandoned her for Jacqueline Kennedy.

Callas's genius flickered again briefly in the mid-1960s, when she sensationally returned to the stage as Tosca, but she soon lost her confidence and perhaps the will to fight too: aside from taking the title role in a (non-operatic) film of *Medea* directed by Pasolini, the last decade of her life was musically barren and deeply unhappy.

What remains are the recordings, in particular the pirate tapes made before her decline set in. Here one can feel the blazing heat she generated in the theatre and the commitment and command she brought to every note she uttered. Nobody but Callas could so grandly seize and shape the arc of a phrase and bring a dramatic situation fiercely to the boil; nobody had a voice which so enthrallingly combined amplitude with flexibility, moulded by the emotionally laden and immediately recognizable dark-hued timbre which became her unique and unmistakable signature.

Rupert Christiansen

RICHARD STRAUSS
1864–1949
the 30-second opera

The first German opera composer

to step out of Wagner's shadow, Richard Strauss had a glittering career as a composer of orchestral music and songs before making his operatic breakthrough with *Salome* (1905) and *Elektra* (1908), for which he adapted existing plays (by Oscar Wilde and Hofmannsthal). With fearsome, dangerous female protagonists and music of daring harmonic freedom and sonic brilliance, both works rode the wave of *fin-de-siècle* fashions to achieve huge popularity. *Elektra* was the start of a collaboration with Hofmannsthal, rare among librettists as being an important literary figure in his own right. Their first operas, *Der Rosenkavalier* and *Ariadne auf Naxos*, explore themes of transience, loss and renewal, with scores that mix neoclassical delicacy, Straussian swagger and the influences of Mozart and Wagner. *Die Frau ohne Schatten* (1917), a complex allegorical fairy tale, was followed in the 1920s by three more operas dealing with marriage, including *Intermezzo* (1923), for which Strauss wrote an autobiographical libretto. On Hofmannsthal's death in 1929, Strauss struggled to find another librettist – a difficulty exacerbated by the cultural politics of the Third Reich – and his later operas, increasingly more reflective than dramatic, are not repertory fixtures, despite his music reaching new levels of refined beauty and vocal writing.

3-SECOND MOTIF
Enfant terrible turned establishment figure, Strauss was a family man who both ruffled feathers and lined his own nest with his many operatic successes.

3-MINUTE ARIA
Berated and admired for sticking to a broadly late-Romantic musical language throughout his long career, Strauss created many of opera's most complex and human characters. He was the husband of a soprano and the son of a horn-player, so his operas invariably feature exquisite writing for the female voice and unusually prominent horn parts in the orchestra.

RELATED TOPICS
See also
ORCHESTRA
page 26

MUSIC DRAMA
page 84

RICHARD WAGNER
page 102

3-SECOND BIOGRAPHIES
FRANZ STRAUSS
1822–1905
Strauss's father, Germany's greatest player of the horn

PAULINE DE AHNA
1863–1950
German soprano who married Strauss in 1894; their famous bickering and genuine love is reflected in several of his operas

HUGO VON HOFMANNSTHAL
1874–1929
Austrian poet and librettist of many of Strauss's operas

30-SECOND TEXT
Hugo Shirley

Strauss was already a famous composer when he made his operatic breakthrough with Salome.

LEOS JANÁČEK
1854–1928

the 30-second opera

Born in humble circumstances in a remote region of what is now the Czech Republic, Janáček matured late as an opera composer (his first masterpiece, *Jenufa*, only premièred when he was 50) and enjoyed little international recognition during his lifetime. Relatively uninterested in the models offered by Wagner and Verdi, he eschewed conventional lyricism and romantic themes. His style can seem rough-edged: influenced by folk traditions (and Slavic composers including Mussorgsky and Dvorak), he brought to his operas abrasive brightness of colour, punchy jagged vigour and a unique emotional directness. A preoccupation with the problem of rendering the inflections and rhythms of ordinary spoken Czech into melodic form means that smoothly shaped tunes play little part in his musical language. Although Janáček's own relationships were unhappy, he had profound empathy with the plight of women, and the fierce Kostelnicka (in *Jenufa*), free-spirited Bytrouska (*The Cunning Little Vixen*) and jaded, sophisticated prima donna Elena (*The Makropoulos Case*) rank among the most vivid and complex of operatic heroines. Yet there is nothing sentimental or maudlin about his compassion for humanity: his music is infused by a vein of anarchic humour and underpinned by a pantheistic creed which finds redemption in nature rather than love.

RELATED TOPICS
See also
VERISMO
page 86

3-SECOND MOTIF
Working outside the Italian-German mainstream, Janáček produced operas of astonishing musical and dramatic originality, often focused on powerful female protagonists.

3-MINUTE ARIA
Janáček's major operas fall into two distinct categories: realistic dramas such as *Jenufa* and *Katya Kabanova*, in which women are the tragic victims of repressive social codes; and those which explore more daringly experimental subject-matter – the amoral animal world in *The Cunning Little Vixen*, space travel in *The Adventures of Mr Broucek*, a tsarist prison camp in *From the House of the Dead*.

3-SECOND BIOGRAPHIES
BEDRICH SMETANA
1824–84
Czech composer of *The Bartered Bridge* and important figure in foundation of the Czech operatic tradition

MODEST MUSSORGSKY
1839–81
Russian composer whose *Boris Godunov* and *Khovanshchina* eschewed Western conventions in search of authentically Russian operatic expression

ANTONIN DVORAK
1841–84
Czech composer who produced 11 operas, the most famous being *Rusalka*

30-SECOND TEXT
Rupert Christiansen

Janáček was one of the first to prefer prose libretti to verse ones, allowing his operas to communicate more naturally and directly.

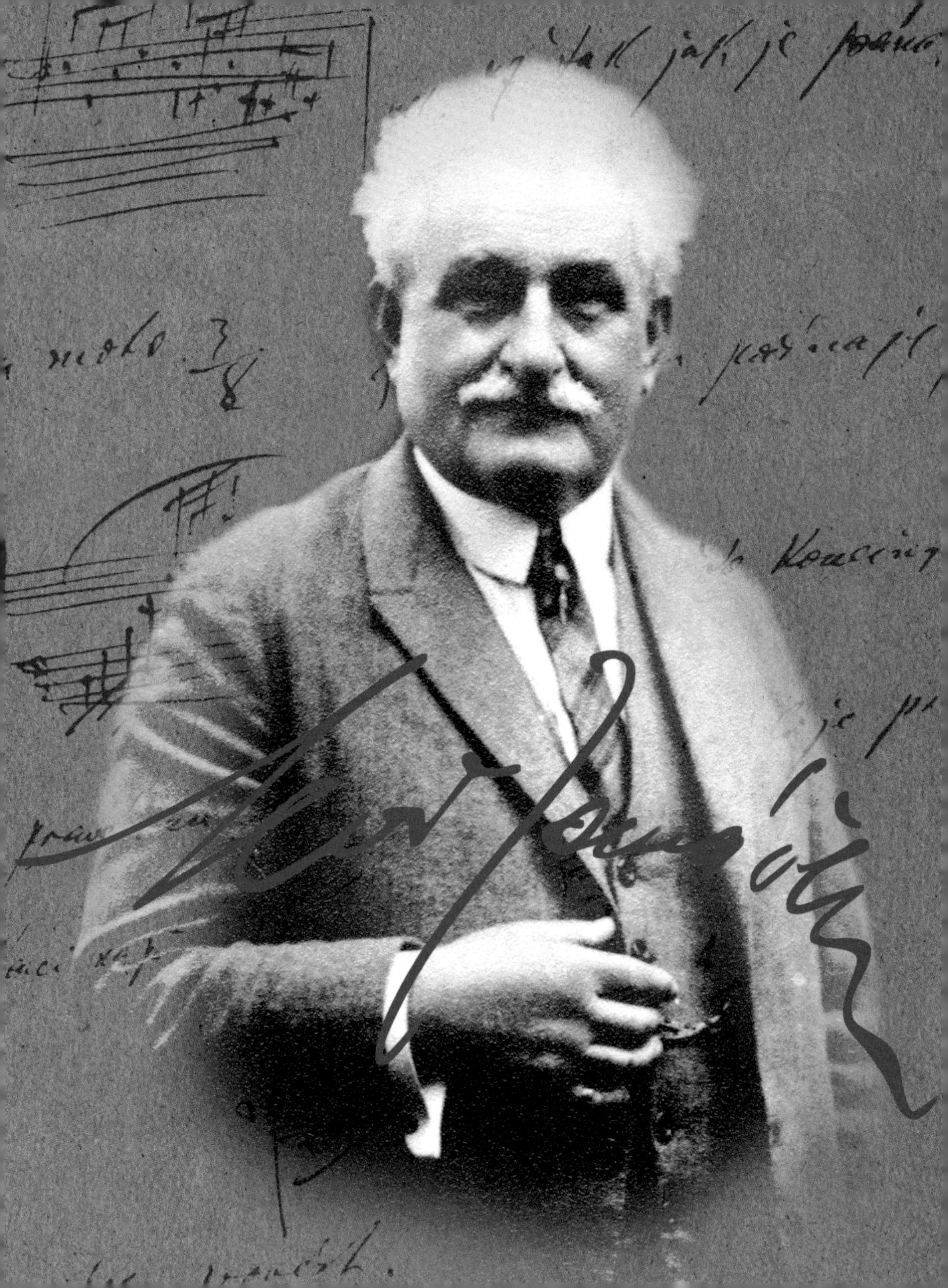

BENJAMIN BRITTEN
1913–1976

the 30-second opera

Britten wrote opera in all shapes

and sizes, on a variety of subjects, because he relished practical challenges. His first major success, the compassionate *Peter Grimes* (1945), focused on the tragedy of an emotionally troubled outsider persecuted by a narrow-minded community. *Billy Budd* and *Gloriana*, full-scale, big-budget operas for Covent Garden followed, but Britten increasingly chose to write for smaller forces and less formal environments. *The Rape of Lucretia*, *Albert Herring* and *The Turn of the Screw* require neither chorus nor large orchestra, making them easy and economical to tour. Basing himself for the latter part of his life in the seaside town of Aldeburgh in his native Suffolk, whose austere coastline he had so expertly evoked in *Peter Grimes*, Britten continued to experiment, bringing greater musical economy and harmonic experimentation – increasingly influenced by sounds of the East – to his later works. *Curlew River* intertwines a Japanese Noh play with the traditions of medieval church drama. His imaginative, light-footed adaptation of Shakespeare's *Midsummer Night's Dream* had wide appeal, but his final masterpiece was an austerely dark-toned treatment of Mann's novella *Death in Venice*. Like many of Britten's operas, it featured a central role for his life-long partner Peter Pears and resonated with uneasy feelings about his attraction to pubescent boys.

3-SECOND MOTIF
No twentieth-century opera composer has had more widespread or immediate impact than Britten, whose work combines fertile musical originality with vivid dramatic energy.

3-MINUTE ARIA
Early in his middle-class childhood, Britten showed prodigious musical talent. Having quickly absorbed lessons from the masters of European modernism, he developed a distinctively personal idiom, writing operas that explore psychologically subtle themes in scores of brilliant clarity and expressive word-setting. Accessible yet complex and innovative, Britten has profoundly influenced a younger generation of composers.

RELATED TOPICS
See also
SCORE
page 18

THE CHORUS
page 42

TWENTIETH CENTURY
page 64

3-SECOND BIOGRAPHIES
PETER PEARS
1910–86
English tenor who was, for more than 40 years, Britten's partner, and for whom the composer wrote many roles

ERIC CROZIER
1914–94
English writer, librettist and co-founder, along with Britten and Peter Pears, of the Aldeburgh Festival in 1948

30-SECOND TEXT
Rupert Christiansen

The shell sculpture on the beach at Aldeburgh serves as a memorial to Britten, who was strongly attached to the land- and seascapes of East Anglia.

VOICES

basso cantante The nearest equivalent to a 'lyrical' bass voice, the basso cantante (literally 'singing bass') will portray noble, thoughtful characters, sing music of long, rolling phrases with a smoothness that a more dramatic, darker-coloured voice might find difficult.

basso profondo This 'deep bass' is a voice capable of plumbing the depths below the bottom of the bass clef, descending as far as the C two octaves below middle C. Famous *basso profondo* roles include Sarastro in *Die Zauberflöte*, while roles such as Don Basilio (*Il barbiere di Siviglia*) and Baron Ochs (*Der Rosenkavalier*) exploit the voice's comic potential.

buffo When talking about voice types, the term *buffo* might be applied to roles – usually, because of operatic convention, for the lower male voices – that are there largely to provide laughs. It might also be used for singers particularly adept at realizing opera's standard comic effects — the sewing-machine-like diction of patter arias, for example. Pure *buffo* roles would include Doctor Bartolo in *Il barbiere di Siviglia* or Leporello, Don Giovanni's servant in Mozart's opera.

coloratura Meaning 'colouring' in Italian, the term coloratura has two related uses. It can refer both to florid and often technically challenging writing for the voice and to the type of singer who is especially expert in executing it. Coloratura sopranos are a voice-type unto themselves, singers whose voices, though sometimes small and light in colour, are supremely agile right up into the vocal stratosphere. Recent years have seen a proliferation of tenors, experts in the florid writing of Rossini in particular, who share the similar characteristics.

Heldentenor The *Heldentenor* (literally, 'hero-tenor') is in some ways the German cousin of the *tenore robusto*. Wagner's heroes (Siegfried in the *Ring* and Tristan) are the original *Heldentenor* roles, requiring not just volume but also enormous stamina, and in which vocal beauty is often sacrificed to dramatic conviction and a basic ability to stay the course across a five-hour evening.

leggiero Meaning simply 'light', this term applies to both the size and the colour of certain voices. Lightness in a voice might mean greater suitability for coloratura, but would restrict a singer too in terms of repertoire – principal roles in operas from after the first couple of decades of the nineteenth century are generally off limits.

lyric In terms of voice classification, the term lyric is applied to singers – more often to sopranos and tenors than other types – whose voices, often the most straightforwardly beautiful if not usually the most penetrating or voluminous, have melodic flexibility and an ability to spin elegant and malleable musical phrases.

spinto The term spinto is short for *lirico-spinto* (meaning 'pushed lyric') and refers to singers who have some of the beauty and elegance of lyrical voices but who can push themselves into more 'dramatic' territory, better able to compete against the larger orchestra that became the norm around the middle of the nineteenth century.

tenore robusto Not the sharpest musical instrument in the box, perhaps, the *tenore robusto* (a subcategory of the 'dramatic' tenor) has a voice that trumps all with its sheer power and stamina, offering thrills of a visceral kind, often portraying men driven more by heart and loins than by head. Verdi's Otello is an unusual example for being such a complex character; Calaf in Puccini's *Turandot* or Canio in Leoncavallo's *Pagliacci* are examples of less reflective roles usually taken by a *tenore robusto*.

tessitura A relatively technical term, tessitura refers to the range (in terms of musical notes) in which the large part of a role lies. One might say, for example, that although a certain singer can sing a role, that the role's tessitura sits a little high (or low) for them.

SOPRANO

the 30-second opera

The highest female voice has

been used throughout operatic history for the heroine in all her many forms. With a range extending up to two octaves (from middle C to top C high above), and occasionally more, the soprano can represent many distinct personas, depending on the size and character of the voice she has: thus the smaller, lighter soubrette would play the maid Susanna in Mozart's *Figaro* or the peasant-girl Zerlina in *Don Giovanni*; the lyric soprano would take on the high-born Countess in *Figaro* or Mimì in Puccini's *La bohème*; while the spinto ('pushed') lyric might appear as Leonora in Verdi's *Il trovatore* or as Aida. Coloratura sopranos sing high and fast – as in many bel canto roles. Striding purposefully around the stage is the dramatic soprano, destined to take on the grandest and most heroic of operatic heroines, such as Wagner's Brünnhilde or Isolde. In Italian 'soprano' is a masculine noun, and the word originally covered not only boy sopranos (or trebles), not usually encountered in opera, but also castratos, who were: they would often play the hero in a higher register until the vogue for the voice ended around the close of the eighteenth century.

3-SECOND MOTIF
Coming in all dramatic shapes and sizes, sopranos dominate opera's glamour stakes. Mostly good girls, though sometimes bad girls, they usually get their man.

3-MINUTE ARIA
Throughout history sopranos have tended to dominate the headlines, with prima donna attitudes typecasting their on- and offstage behaviour. Artists such as the legendary Jenny Lind or Adelina Patti could also command the highest fees. In the 1950s opera fans divided into supporters of Maria Callas and Renata Tebaldi, at least until Joan Sutherland came along to complicate the picture. More recently Birgit Nilsson, Montserrat Caballé, Angela Gheorghiu and Anna Netrebko have all achieved full diva status.

RELATED TOPICS
See also
JENNY LIND
page 44

BEL CANTO
page 76

MARIA CALLAS
page 110

3-SECOND BIOGRAPHIES
RENATA TEBALDI
1922–2004
Italian soprano, one of the post-war era greats, who represented the aristocratic Italian vocal traditioin

ANGELA GHEORGHIU
1965–
Romanian soprano, who married her second husband, tenor Roberto Alagna, on the stage of the Met in New York

30-SECOND TEXT
George Hall

Sopranos have been the opera's most obvious stars, and are often the focus of attention off stage as well as on.

MEZZO-SOPRANO/ CONTRALTO

the 30-second opera

The mezzo-soprano ('medium' soprano) is pitched lower than the soprano, and when they sing in duet will invariably sing beneath her. Often the difference depends less on range than on tessitura: whether the bulk of the part lies in higher or lower vocal territory. Differently sized voices undertake roles of different characters: a lyric mezzo might sing the faithful maid Suzuki in Puccini's *Madama Butterfly*, the dramatic mezzo the grandly regal Amneris in Verdi's *Aida*. Far more so than in the case of the soprano, mezzos have inherited the parts once sung by alto castrati: nowadays they regularly undertake roles such as Julius Caesar in Handel's *Giulio Cesare in Egitto*. In an extension of this tradition, mezzos play many juvenile leads, like the principal boy in pantomime: thus Cherubino in Mozart's *Figaro* and Octavian in Strauss's *Der Rosenkavalier* are both for mezzos, with dressing and moving as a boy in 'trouser roles' becoming essential skills. Paradoxically, they also play self-consciously sexy female roles, such as Bizet's Carmen or Delilah in Saint-Saëns' *Samson et Dalila*, often with a soprano as their rival in love. Rarer these days, and lower than the mezzo-soprano, the contralto specializes in such roles as Ulrica the fortune-teller in Verdi's *Un ballo in maschera* and Erda in Wagner's *Ring*.

3-SECOND MOTIF
Mezzos can be sexy girls or boys, often (as the former) rivalling the soprano for the tenor's affections – though with mixed results.

3-MINUTE ARIA
Mezzo-sopranos and contraltos have played second fiddle to sopranos in terms of wider fame – with exceptions. Many nineteenth-century composers were inspired to write for stars such as Maria Malibran and her sister Pauline Viardot, while Kathleen Ferrier created the title role of Britten's *The Rape of Lucretia* in 1946. More recently Dame Janet Baker, Marilyn Horne and Cecilia Bartoli have flown the mezzo flag with distinction.

RELATED TOPICS
See also
GIOACHINO ROSSINI
page 98

SOPRANO
page 122

3-SECOND BIOGRAPHIES
KATHLEEN FERRIER
1912–53
English contralto most famous, perhaps, for her performances in Gluck's *Orpheus*

DAME JANET BAKER
1933–
English mezzo who triumphed in Gluck's *Orpheus* and Donizetti's *Mary Stuart*

MARILYN HORNE
1934–
US mezzo-soprano, known as 'General Horne' from the number of helmeted ancient warriors she played in what were formerly castrato roles

---

30-SECOND TEXT
George Hall

Contraltos and mezzos are frequently cast in roles that, in the past, would have gone to castrato singers.

COUNTERTENOR
the 30-second opera

The countertenor is a male singer

whose vocal range typically extends two octaves from the G below middle C, approximately equivalent to that of the contralto. Singing in head voice, or falsetto, in all but the lowest notes, the countertenor is largely used in Baroque opera, in roles written for the castrati: singers who were castrated in childhood to preserve the pitch of their unbroken voices. The practice was largely restricted to Italy, where the church turned a blind eye to the number of boy trebles who were operated upon as the result of fictitious accidents. The castrato fell from operatic fashion in the nineteenth century and following renewed popularity of early opera in the twentieth century, castrato roles, albeit sometimes sung by mezzo sopranos, started to be taken by countertenors, considered by some to represent a more 'authentic' option. Since Benjamin Britten created the role of Oberon in *A Midsummer Night's Dream* for Alfred Deller in 1960, composers have warmed to the other-worldly sound of the voice. Apollo in Britten's *Death in Venice* (1973), the title role of Philip Glass's *Akhnaten* (1983), the sisters in Péter Eötvös's *Three Sisters* (1997), the role of The Boy in George Benjamin's *Written on Skin* (2012) and the Handel revival have seen the modern countertenor consolidate his place on the stage.

3-SECOND MOTIF
Once heard only in church music, the countertenor voice is now prized in performances of Baroque and contemporary opera. With increased exposure, technique and tone have been refined.

3-MINUTE ARIA
From Alfred Deller's debut as Britten's Oberon, the countertenor has been transformed from a novelty to a voice-type as affecting and agile as any other. James Bowman led the second generation of operatic countertenors. His successors include David Daniels, Andreas Scholl, Iestyn Davies, Bejun Mehta and Philippe Jaroussky.

RELATED TOPICS
See also
FARINELLI
page 24

BAROQUE
page 54

GEORG FRIDERIC HANDEL
page 94

BENJAMIN BRITTEN
page 116

THE HERO
page 144

3-SECOND BIOGRAPHIES
ALFRED DELLER
1912–79
English countertenor who transformed the profile of his voice type in opera

DAVID DANIELS
1966–
American countertenor, the first to give a recital at Carnegie Hall, who epitomizes the modern superstar

30-SECOND TEXT
Anna Picard

The countertenor has in recent years become a fixture in new operas.

TENOR

the 30-second opera

Though it found an honourable

place in some of the earliest operas – the title-role of Monteverdi's *Orfeo* (1607), for instance – the tenor voice achieved a dominant position as the inevitable personification of the young hero in the early nineteenth century with the decline of the castrato. The highest male voice regularly used, it is heard at its happiest and most characteristic in the octave between middle C (C_4) to tenor top C (C_5), where many arias find their natural point of climax; such high (and occasionally higher) notes are flaunted shamelessly in the operas of Rossini, Bellini and Donizetti. It was in a performance of Rossini's *Guillaume Tell* in Lucca in 1831 that the early nineteenth-century tenor Gilbert Duprez first attempted a high C from the chest, rather than in *falsetto*, driving the audience into a frenzy; such viscerally thrilling notes have been a mainstay of the tenor armoury ever since. The *leggiero* (or light) and lyric tenor voices (as encountered in Rossini and Donizetti) often develop into the *spinto* (or 'pushed') tenor, suited to more heroic roles (such as Radames in Verdi's *Aida*); Italians use the term tenore *robusto* for the equivalent (eg Verdi's Otello) of the Wagner roles for which the Germans use the word *Heldentenor*.

RELATED TOPICS
See also
ENRICO CARUSO
page 62

SOPRANO
page 122

PLÁCIDO DOMINGO
page 130

THE HERO
page 144

3-SECOND BIOGRAPHIES
GILBERT DUPREZ
1806–96
French tenor

LUCIANO PAVAROTTI
1935–2007
Italian tenor who, with Plácido Domingo and José Carreras, performed as The Three Tenors in the 1990s and early 2000s

JOSÉ CARRERAS
1946–
Catalan tenor

30-SECOND TEXT
George Hall

If the soprano has always been the heroine, the tenor was only really established as the hero in the nineteenth century.

3-SECOND MOTIF
With tension inherent in the tone itself, the tenor's realization of the hero's emotional highpoints provide opera's most exciting experience.

3-MINUTE ARIA
The tenor became opera's regular male star in the nineteenth century, with the Italian Enrico Caruso the first to become a recording star in the twentieth, succeeded by his compatriot Beniamino Gigli. From their initial joint appearance at the World Cup Final in Rome in 1990, the Three Tenors – Plácido Domingo, Luciano Pavarotti and José Carreras – became media superstars; their successors include Juan Diego Flórez, Joseph Calleja and Jonas Kaufmann.

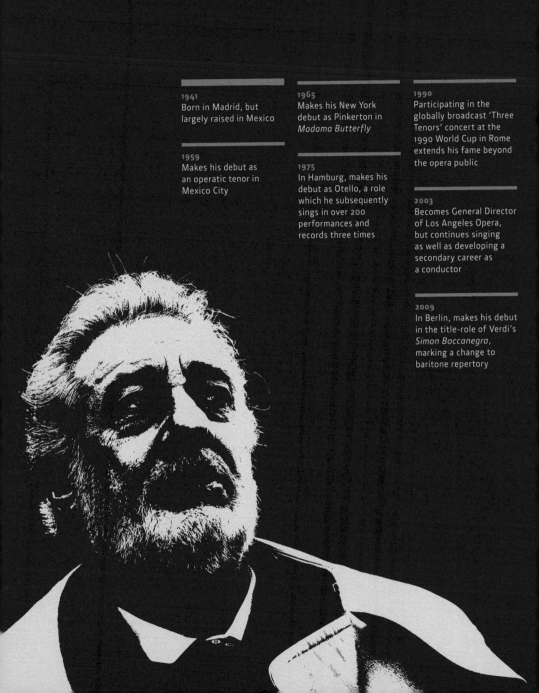

1941
Born in Madrid, but largely raised in Mexico

1959
Makes his debut as an operatic tenor in Mexico City

1965
Makes his New York debut as Pinkerton in *Madama Butterfly*

1975
In Hamburg, makes his debut as Otello, a role which he subsequently sings in over 200 performances and records three times

1990
Participating in the globally broadcast 'Three Tenors' concert at the 1990 World Cup in Rome extends his fame beyond the opera public

2003
Becomes General Director of Los Angeles Opera, but continues singing as well as developing a secondary career as a conductor

2009
In Berlin, makes his debut in the title-role of Verdi's *Simon Boccanegra*, marking a change to baritone repertory

PLÁCIDO DOMINGO

With a career spanning more than half a century, nearly 150 roles, over 3,500 performances and 100 recordings, tenor Plácido Domingo has a fair claim to rank as the most versatile and prolific figure in operatic history.

Starting with a focus on the more standard lyrical aspects of the Verdi and Puccini repertory, he gradually extended his range to more heroic challenges, such as Samson in *Samson et Dalila*, Hermann in *The Queen of Spades*, Siegmund in *Die Walküre* and the title-role in *Parsifal*, as well as making occasional forays into operetta, the Baroque and new opera.

Such was his non-stop schedule and relentless globe-trotting that soprano Birgit Nilsson cynically quipped that 'Placido may sing beautifully in five languages, but he doesn't seem to know the word for "No" in any of them.' 'If I rest, I rust,' he would retort.

His major artistic achievement was undoubtedly his interpretation of Verdi's *Otello*. Although others may have invested this demanding role with a more intense sense of emotional agony, Domingo's reading had a nobility and sincerity which made it deeply moving, complemented by singing of unfailing control and sensitive musicality.

These qualities characterized all his interpretations – to the point that sterner critics found them somewhat predictable, undifferentiated and imperturbable. The great majority preferred to celebrate the expansive generosity of his phrasing, the steady glow of his tone and astonishingly high level of consistency, underpinned by his tall, handsome stage presence, sterling professionalism and warm personality. He seldom cancelled, he always obliged.

As Domingo approached his seventieth birthday, his top notes were no longer reliably produced and he began to play baritone roles concentrated on a middle register which had always been the most solid part of his voice. His success in this risky venture was remarkable.

Beyond singing, his ambition remains insatiable and his altruistic contribution to the cause of opera immense. He took (with mixed results) senior management roles with opera companies in both Washington, D.C. and Los Angeles and became a decent if humdrum conductor of Puccini. As well as much informal encouragement of aspirants to the profession, he generously endowed Operalia, a prestigious competition which launched many young singers into stardom. Above all, he serves tirelessly as opera's greatest ambassador and public face, ever ready to appear at fund-raising galas or receive prizes and medals from crowned and presidential heads. Such honours – and the fortune which attends them – are richly merited.

Rupert Christiansen

BARITONE/ BASS-BARITONE

the 30-second opera

The baritone is often the most

complex character in an opera. Falling between bass and tenor, his range allows him some of the gravitas of the lower voice and some of the glamour of the higher one – though not enough of either to earn him the status of hero; his role nevertheless often rivals the tenor, usually in love. The standard eternal triangle of the operatic scenario goes: soprano and tenor love each other, but the baritone gets in the way. Examples are Verdi's *La traviata*, where soprano Violetta loves tenor Alfredo but his baritone father Giorgio forces her to give him up, or Puccini's *Tosca*, where soprano Tosca loves tenor Cavaradossi but baritone Scarpia has him tortured and shot, and tries to rape her. Baritones often play the villain, pure and simple. Although the voice existed much earlier (the Count in Mozart's *Figaro* is a classic baritone role), it grew exponentially in the nineteenth century, with the fascination Verdi developed for it as a vehicle for acting, especially in such instances as Simon Boccanegra, Iago in *Otello* or Falstaff. Wagner, too, made the most of its expressive potential in a plethora of roles (such as Wotan in *the Ring*), which are regularly sung by the bass-baritone.

RELATED TOPIC
See also
GIUSEPPE VERDI
page 100

3-SECOND MOTIF
Baritones are often bad, occasionally mad and almost invariably dangerous to know – especially if you're a tenor or a soprano.

3-MINUTE ARIA
Perhaps because they often play the unglamorous characters who fail to get the girl, baritones have not regularly attracted the fame tenors seem to achieve with greater ease. But Verdi loved the voice, writing splendid parts for singers such as Giorgio Ronconi, Felice Varesi and Victor Maurel, all of whom could act as well as sing; as, too, can modern performers including Sir Thomas Allen, Simon Keenlyside and the great bass-baritone Bryn Terfel.

3-SECOND BIOGRAPHIES
VICTOR MAUREL
1848–1923
French baritone who created roles in operas by Verdi

THOMAS HAMPSON
1955–
American baritone of immense versatility, scholar and educator

BRYN TERFEL
1965–
Welsh bass-baritone, a leading singer of Wagnerian roles in particular

30-SECOND TEXT
George Hall

The men in the middle: baritone roles can be among opera's most complex, mixing heroism and gravitas.

BASS

the 30-second opera

The lowest male voice, the bass regularly represents an authority figure in opera. Kings (Philip II of Spain in Verdi's *Don Carlos*, England's Henry VIII in Donizetti's *Anna Bolena*), high priests (Ramfis in Verdi's *Aida*, Oroveso in Bellini's *Norma*), gods (Pluto in Monteverdi's *Orfeo*) or oracles (the Oracle of Neptune in Mozart's *Idomeneo*) all have their power and status confirmed by the lowest notes in their vocal range, which drops nearly two octaves from middle C. Philip II, or the aged nobleman Silva in Verdi's *Ernani*, are examples of the *basso cantante* ('singing bass'), more lyrical in expression than dramatic bass roles such as the guilt-ridden Tsar Boris in Mussorgsky's *Boris Godunov* or the evil magician Klingsor in Wagner's *Parsifal*. The *buffo* ('comic') bass specializes in rapid patter songs and general buffoonery in such roles as the crusty senior Dr Bartolo in Rossini's *Il barbiere di Siviglia*, or his belatedly amorous equivalent in the title role of Donizetti's *Don Pasquale*. A few notes lower even than the standard bass lies the *basso profondo* ('deep bass'), typified by Sarastro in Mozart's *Die Zauberflöte* and Osmin in his *Die Entführung aus dem Serail*, both of whom sing some of the lowest notes ever written for the human voice.

RELATED TOPICS
See also
FYODOR CHALIAPIN
page 80

BARITONE/BASS-BARITONE
page 132

THE BUFFOON
page 150

GODS & MONSTERS
page 152

3-SECOND BIOGRAPHIES
EZIO PINZA
1892–1957
Handsome Italian bass who, following his retirement from opera, created the role of Emile de Becque in Rodgers & Hammerstein's *South Pacific*

SIR JOHN TOMLINSON
1946–
Leading English bass, whose credits include appearances at every Bayreuth Festival between 1988 and 2006

30-SECOND TEXT
George Hall

The singer with the lowest range, the bass is often the voice of authority, experience and reason.

3-SECOND MOTIF
Basses provide the foundation stones of many plots and are usually deferred to by sopranos and tenors: the general rule is, don't mess with them.

3-MINUTE ARIA
Considered one of the finest actors of his day, Fyodor Chaliapin was a legendary Boris Godunov and also created Massenet's *Don Quichotte*. The Italian Ezio Pinza was a superb Don Giovanni – both on and off the stage, apparently. In our time Sir John Tomlinson has conquered virtually every standard bass role and created several more, notably by Sir Harrison Birtwistle.

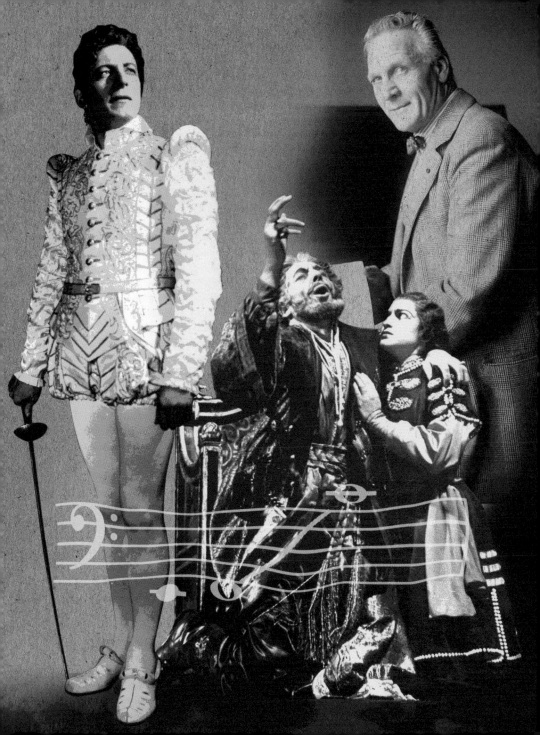

CHARACTERS

catharsis A term that goes back to ancient Greek theories regarding the beneficial (and, literally, cleansing and purging) qualities of art – and of tragedy in particular. Arguably opera, with its many constituent elements, can offer a sense of catharsis unlike any other art form, and certainly one close to that described by Aristotle in the Greek drama that opera has, throughout its history, so often sought to emulate.

commedia dell'arte A sixteenth- and seventeenth-century form of (professional) Italian comic theatre whose conventional characters (often cross-dressing) and stock storylines were a powerful influence on *opera buffa*. Such targets of *Commedia dell'arte*'s ridicule as old men's desire for much younger women are common in comic opera, as are the types of servant girls, soldiers, cunning servants and old buffoons. *Commedia dell'arte* performances would often include music, too.

diva Translating literally as 'goddess' (the male equivalent is 'divo'), the word diva reflects the importance opera-lovers attached to stars from the very earliest period in opera; the fact that this word (along with 'prima donna' – meaning, literally, 'first lady') is also current today in other musical contexts suggests how little celebrity culture has changed.

Madonna–whore dichotomy Sigmund Freud argued that some men suffer from what he termed the 'Madonna–whore complex': they were able only to view women as belonging to one of those two extreme categories. It is perhaps no accident that opera – an art form historically produced almost exclusively by men, and which itself often dealt in extremes – would sometimes reflect its own Madonna–whore complex, positioning its female characters at one or other end of the dichotomy to emphasise either the drama or, in some cases, the moral lessons it was trying to convey. Recent writing on opera (including much by ground-breaking feminist critics) has exposed this tendency, while some productions have actively sought to question or invert the black-and-white characterizations that some operas suggest.

patter aria A patter aria or song is one that exploits singers' linguistic ability, cramming words together in very quick succession for comic effect. Although there are earlier examples, it only became a standard device towards the end of the eighteenth century, and became a speciality of Rossini, in particular – a prime example in *Il barbiere di Siviglia* is Dr Bartolo's 'A un dottor della mia sorte', but Figaro's famous 'Largo al factotum' from the same opera also concludes with a word-packed rush to the finish line. The patter song was also a staple of Gilbert and Sullivan: *The Pirates of Penzance*'s 'I am the very model of a modern major general', for example, or the so-called Patter Trio from *Ruddigore*, which gently mocks the device and concludes: 'This particularly rapid, unintelligible patter/Isn't generally heard, and if it is it doesn't matter!'

soubrette A French word meaning 'servant girl', and in operatic terms is often exactly that: such sparky, resourceful and attractive characters as Susanna in Mozart's *Le nozze di Figaro* or Zerlina in *Don Giovanni*. The word might also be used to describe a singer whose voice is suited to these roles: bright-sounding, relatively light sopranos with, ideally, plenty of beauty and bell-like ping.

travesti/trouser roles Women playing men (in 'trouser roles', sometimes also called 'breeches parts') and men playing women (a phenomenon for which the term *en travesty* – 'in disguise' – is usually although not exclusively reserved) is nothing unusual in opera. Until the first quarter of the nineteenth century, young men would often be embodied by sopranos or mezzos (Cherubino in *Le nozze di Figaro*, for example, or Bellini's Romeo in *I Capuletti e i Montecchi*), while in early opera men would often also play women, a famous early example being the Nurse Arnalta in Monteverdi's *L'incoronazione di Poppea*. At other times, practical considerations dictated such choices, with castratos sometimes singing female roles in parts of seventeenth- and eighteenth-century Italy when women were not allowed to appear on stage. In later opera, on the other hand, gender-crossing casting was often made for specific aesthetic reasons, such as with Octavian in Strauss' *Der Rosenkavalier* or the (tenor) Mad Woman in Britten's *Curlew River*.

THE ANGEL

the 30-second opera

Prior to the nineteenth century,

operatic heroines came in various guises. From around 1820, however, gutsy types like the warrior queen were waning, replaced by the archetypal young, innocent heroine who lives only for love, always sung by a soprano. This shift was in part the consequence of a turn towards operatic tragedy, with the 'angel' character becoming the sacrificial victim. However, it was also prompted by broader changes in attitudes towards women and their representation: in much nineteenth-century literature and art, women were constructed either as 'angels' or 'whores'. Operas, like other artworks, served a didactic purpose, promoting passive, virtuous and pious female behaviour: many operatic 'angels' sing a prayer scene, especially in Italian opera. These characters inevitably begin whiter than white, although some are sullied during the course of events, even (in the case of *Lucia di Lammermoor*) driven to terrible crimes. Conversely, former 'fallen' women with 'hearts of gold', such as Violetta in *La traviata*, are sometimes redeemed by the love of a good man. Either way, the operatic angel is doomed: nineteenth-century operas revelled in the suffering and death of beautiful young women. The angel's function within opera is effectively to elicit from audiences maximum empathy and catharsis.

RELATED TOPICS
See also
ROMANTIC
page 58

GIUSEPPE VERDI
page 100

GIACOMO PUCCINI
page 108

SOPRANO
page 122

THE FEMME FATALE
page 142

30-SECOND TEXT
Alexandra Wilson

3-SECOND MOTIF
A throwback to a less enlightened age, the submissive angel disturbs modern sensibilities, but could be considered to gain some empowerment through her vocal virtuosity.

3-MINUTE ARIA
Operatic 'angels' are, mostly, passive characters who have little autonomy from the men around them; their would-be lovers and even their own fathers humiliate, mistreat and murder them. The self-sacrificial angel who commits suicide in the name of an unworthy man is a recurring type: Cio-Cio San (*Madama Butterfly*) kills herself after being abandoned by a cad, while Gilda (*Rigoletto*) offers herself up to a hired assassin to save a philandering duke.

Opera loves to portray the unsullied, angelic heroine; and it loves even more to show her undoing.

SONGS *in* the Opera Call'd PYRRHUS *and* DEMETRIUS

THE FEMME FATALE

the 30-second opera

The *femme fatale* and the angel

sit at opposite ends of the nineteenth century's Madonna–whore dichotomy. Where the angel is chaste, the *femme fatale* is tainted; where the angel is submissive, the *femme fatale* does her own thing. She cares little for the men she seduces but is herself the object of obsessive love: the term fatal denotes the fact that she typically corrupts a good man with her beauty and cunning and drags him to his doom. Composers sometimes juxtaposed the two characters within a single opera to establish a stark contrast between the ideal woman a nineteenth-century man was supposed to marry and the fallen woman he must avoid at all costs. In reality, however, numerous 'respectable' middle-class men of the nineteenth century lived double lives and the operatic *femme fatale* was undoubtedly intended to titillate with her sensual music and provocative dances. Whereas angels are invariably sung by sopranos, *femmes fatales* may be either sopranos or mezzo-sopranos, the lower range of the mezzo voice denoting the *femme fatale*'s earthiness, removing her from the angel's ethereal sphere. A *femme fatale* could never be allowed to triumph – this character type is invariably killed off for her transgressions at the end of an opera.

RELATED TOPICS

See also
ROMANTIC
page 58

TWENTIETH CENTURY
page 64

SOPRANO
page 122

MEZZO-SOPRANO/CONTRALTO
page 124

THE ANGEL
page 140

30-SECOND TEXT
Alexandra Wilson

3-SECOND MOTIF
Femme fatale figures feature most frequently in Italian, French and German operas of the later nineteenth and early twentieth centuries.

3-MINUTE ARIA
The operatic *femme fatale* was often rendered even more seductive by being removed from the recognizable environment of the audience members. The biblical *femmes fatales* Dalila (in Saint-Saëns' opera) and Salome (Strauss) were distanced from 'real life' both temporally and geographically. A more modern and realistic, but equally exoticized femme fatale was Bizet's Carmen, a gritty factory-worker from Seville who tempts an honest soldier, setting him on a course towards self-destruction.

From Dalila to Salome and Carmen, the operatic femme fatale is sexy and exotic, often proving literally fatal to those who succumb to her charms.

THE HERO

the 30-second opera

In the earliest court operas of the seventeenth century, composers sought to flatter patrons by likening them to heroes of ancient Greek legend: Monteverdi's *Orfeo* for example. Heroes of Baroque and Classical opera (whether mythological or historical figures, such as Handel's *Giulio Cesare*) were often genuinely heroic, exhibiting military daring, honourable acts and sometimes a willingness to sacrifice themselves for the greater good. By the Romantic era, literary heroes had become brooding wanderers; Wagner's epic heroes, drawn from medieval legend, developed out of this model. Later, however, the quest for operatic realism led composers to move away from idealized character types. Despite an ongoing veneration of heroic manliness in nineteenth-century society, composers were by this time often more interested in depicting flawed, psychologically interesting characters than in creating male role models. The so-called operatic heroes of the later nineteenth and twentieth centuries may be convincing romantic leads with strong passions but often lack nobility and courage; even military men such as Don José (*Carmen*), Otello or Pinkerton (*Madama Butterfly*) behave in ways that could hardly be described as heroic. Very often, in opera of this period, it is the heroine not the hero who elicits our sympathies and exhibits qualities of dignity and inner strength.

3-SECOND MOTIF
In earlier operas, hero and heroine were often reunited at the end, whereas by the nineteenth century it was probable that one or both would perish.

3-MINUTE ARIA
The voice types associated with heroism changed over the course of opera's history. During the seventeenth and eighteenth centuries, it was the castrato voice that was considered heroic. As this voice type declined in the early nineteenth century, heroes were sometimes played by women dressed as men ('travesty roles') but increasingly it was the tenor who took on the heroic mantle.

RELATED TOPICS
See also
FARINELLI
page 24

ENRICO CARUSO
page 62

TENOR
page 128

GODS & MONSTERS
page 152

30-SECOND TEXT
Alexandra Wilson

Out of the uncomplicated heroes of early operas grew the complex, tortured and compromised heroes of later Wagner and Verdi.

1969
Born Joyce Flaherty
in Kansas

1998
Begins her professional
career after winning
prizes in several major
competitions

2000
Makes debut at La Scala
in title-role of Rossini's
La Cenerentola

2005
Makes debut at
Metropolitan Opera
as Cherubino in
Le Nozze di Figaro

2009
Hits the headlines when
she breaks her fibula on
stage during *Il Barbiere di
Siviglia* at Covent Garden
– and finishes the
performance on crutches

2013
Reaches a global audience
of millions when she
sings at the BBC's *Last
Night of the Proms* at the
Royal Albert Hall

2014
Sings the national
anthem in the Kauffmann
Stadium in Kansas City
before the final game of
the 2014 World Series

JOYCE DIDONATO

Over the past fifty years, the singing of the mezzo-soprano music of Handel, Mozart and Rossini has been handsomely served by a succession of great singers including Teresa Berganza, Marilyn Horne, Janet Baker, Ann Murray and Cecilia Bartoli, who have combined mercurial elasticity of technique with a brightness of tone that could almost cause them to be mistaken for sopranos.

The youngest of this line is Joyce DiDonato. A cheerful, energetic blonde from the American Midwest, as happy to sing 'Over the Rainbow' as a baroque aria, she radiates a fresh, ingenuous personality which, in an age impatient with old-school prima donna pomposity, has made her hugely popular.

But she is no lightweight: having struggled through an arduous training and many early setbacks, she has developed a magnificent armoury of vocal skills that serves her deeply sensitive insight into period style and gives her singing a textbook perfection in terms of clarity, articulation and smoothness. For meticulous attention to the precise detail of a score, DiDonato is unrivalled.

Alongside Handelian heroines (such as Alcina) and Mozartian trouser roles (such as Idamante in *Idomeneo*), DiDonato has made a speciality of the bel canto repertory – notably Rossini's *La Cenerentola*, *Il Barbiere di Siviglia*, *La Donna del Lago*, Bellini's *I Capuleti e I Montecchi* and Donizetti's *Maria Stuarda*. In lesser throats, this music can become merely the vehicle for empty virtuosity, but DiDonato brings the characters vividly to sympathetic and credible life, sculpting the vocal lines with deep imagination and impeccable taste.

Recently, she has also shown interest in French composers and high romantic operas by Massenet and Berlioz will probably feature as she reaches what should be the peak of her career. However, the innately modest dimensions of her voice – it doesn't expand to chesty blasts – are likely to preclude her entering heavier Italian or German territory.

DiDonato is a thoroughly modern diva, who has made enthusiastic use of social media and the press to promote her crusading advocacy of opera – not as a museum art form for an élite nor as something which needs dumbing-down for the masses, but as vividly expressive musical drama. 'Selling opera on the basis that it's superficially cool and hip – that is so phoney', she said in one interview. She herself has no need of gimmicks: her sublime artistry and unaffected charm combine to make her one of the great stars of twenty-first-century opera.

Rupert Christiansen

THE RIVAL
the 30-second opera

RELATED TOPICS
See also
MEZZO-SOPRANO/
CONTRALTO
page 124

BARITONE/BASS-BARITONE
page 132

THE FEMME FATALE
page 142

30-SECOND TEXT
Hugo Shirley

3-SECOND MOTIF
In opera the tenor and the soprano are in love; it's a safe bet that a jealous mezzo or baritone is scheming in the wings.

3-MINUTE ARIA
In nineteenth-century opera, the fate of the rival tells much about the differences between the national schools: in Italian opera, emotions become less controllable and the results increasingly fatal; Wagner's operas, by contrast, increasingly influenced by pessimistic philosophy, started to encourage noble renunciation.

'A tenor and soprano want to make love,' runs George Bernard Shaw's mischievous summary of operatic plots, 'but are prevented from doing so by a baritone.' Operatic love triangles often have their own rules, where rivals tend to be mezzos or baritones: the former typically with swaying hips and seductive tunes to lure the tenor from his angelic beloved; the latter might remain frustrated – despite having power, money or charm – or be motivated by their own sense of injustice. One of opera's greatest rivals is the police chief Scarpia, who in Puccini's *Tosca*, tortures the tenor, Cavaradossi, to try to have his way with Tosca. Scarpia even compares himself to Iago (brought to the operatic stage by Verdi in *Otello*) whose scheming is unusual and all the more chilling for being motivated by nothing. In Verdi's *Il trovatore* Count Di Luna is perhaps more conventional, until he learns that his rival in love, Manrico, is his brother: it's a long story. Mezzo rivals are more complicated, often reflecting the dangerous underside of the Madonna–whore dichotomy that so occupied opera, especially in the nineteenth century. Most famously, Bizet's Carmen crosses the line from mere rival to all-encompassing femme fatale. Representative of a more scheming sort might be the spurned Princesse de Bouillon in Francesco Cilea's *Adriana Lecouvreur*, who serves her revenge cold, delivering Adriana a bunch of poisoned flowers.

Representing the pivotal corner of any love triangle, the rival is the essential driver of many an operatic plot.

THE BUFFOON

the 30-second opera

Although naturally closely related to
the comedy characters and associated conventions
in spoken theatre – and especially in the Italian
tradition of *commedia dell' arte* – the operatic
buffoon benefits further from the humorous
possibilities of music: the so-called patter aria,
in particular, becomes a staple in nineteenth-
century comic opera. Ribald comedy was an
essential element of some of the earliest operas,
however, with a tradition developing early for
cynical, bawdy nurses, often performed today drag
(Arnalta in Monteverdi's *L'incoronazione di Poppea*
is a prime example). Such things had little place in
the more formalized, high-flown Baroque genres,
but of course the buffoon came back with a
vengeance in *opera buffa*. Stock characters and
situations evolved, often involving fusty, over-
protective parents or guardians intent on marrying
younger offspring to wealthy but unappealing
partners, or elderly men with over-optimistic
amorous ambitions. Donizetti's *Don Pasquale*
combines all these elements, while Dr Bartolo (in
Rossini's *Il barbiere di Siviglia*) is a fine example of
operatic pomposity – easily outsmarted by the
barber Figaro. As the nineteenth century
progressed, operatic buffoons tended increasingly
to be representatives of outmoded institutions or
social orders. They also took on a political
dimension in more nationalistic folk comedies (for
example Beckmesser in Wagner's *Meistersinger*).

3-SECOND MOTIF
Often old and easy to
outsmart, operatic
buffoons tend to be
further burdened by
music that is deliberately
pedantic, old-fashioned
or both.

3-MINUTE ARIA
The darker side of these
buffoons, and the
well-known 'tears of a
clown' idea, was explored
in Leoncavallo's *Pagliacci*.
In his famous aria, 'Vesti
la giubba' (On with the
motley), the betrayed
clown Canio declares the
show must go on. He ends
up, however, stabbing his
wife and her lover, and
declaring 'La commedia
è finita'.

RELATED TOPICS
See also
BAROQUE
page 54

OPERA BUFFA
page 74

30-SECOND TEXT
Hugo Shirley

*The witty and wise
title character of
Verdi's* **Falstaff**
*concludes by singing:
'All the world's a joke'.*

GODS & MONSTERS

the 30-second opera

The extravagant theatricality of opera has often required the need for depictions of the supernatural. Early opera's concern with Greek myth invariably resulted in the portrayal of gods, where they would often – especially in the more irreverent Venetian operas – be given some pointedly human weaknesses. The implied critique of authority was thinly veiled. In later opera, written under aristocratic or royal patronage and often guided by strict regulations of what could or could not be portrayed on stage (at various points, biblical subjects have been banned) deities would be represented by deep-voiced priests – say Zacarria in Verdi's *Nabucco* or, in a character who embodies criticism of religious fundamentalism, the Grand Inquisitor in *Don Carlos*. In Wagner's Ring cycle the operatic god Wotan shows himself to be all too human: his divinity is tarnished by lying, philandering, impatience and a tendency to break hastily-made promises. The flipside was the operatic devil, memorably portrayed as suave, persuasive Mephistopheles characters in Berlioz's *Damnation de Faust*, Gounod's *Faust* and Boito's *Mefistofele* and Meyerbeer's *Robert le Diable*. These characters were doubly fascinating: sung by dark-voiced, booming basses, often hailing from exotic eastern Europe or Russia, they invariably served as catalysts in the downfall of an angelic heroine.

RELATED TOPICS
See also
BEGINNINGS
page 52

GRAND OPÉRA
page 78

RICHARD WAGNER
page 102

BASS
page 134

3-SECOND BIOGRAPHY
JOHANN WOLFGANG
VON GOETHE
1749–1832
German poet and playwright, author of *Faust* on which several operas were based

30-SECOND TEXT
Hugo Shirley

3-SECOND MOTIF
The devil might always get the best tunes, but opera's gods can sometimes make the richest characters.

3-MINUTE ARIA
The way embodiments of authority – gods, priests, kings – are portrayed on the operatic stage can tell us a great deal about how opera engaged in criticism of the political status quo. Operatic monsters and devils, on the other hand, were a speciality of nineteenth-century Parisian opera, allowing for both titillation and exhilarating special effects.

Wagner's Wotan, one of the most famous operatic gods, is also one of the most complex and moving characters in all opera.

RESOURCES

BOOKS

Aspects of Wagner
Brian Magee
(Oxford University Press, 1988)

Believing in Opera
Tom Sutcliffe
(Princeton University Press, 2014)

The Birth of an Opera
Michael Rose
(Norton, 2013)

Divas and Scholars
Philip Gossett
(University of Chicago Press, 2006)

English National Opera Guides series
(Overture Publishing, 2011)

From the Score to the Stage
Evan Baker
(University of Chicago Press, 2013)

The Guilded Stage
Daniel Snowman
(Atlantic Books, 2010)

*A History of Opera: The Last Four
Hundred Years*
Carolyn Abbate and Roger Parker
(Allen Lane, 2012)

(Penguin, 2012)
Mozart and His Operas
David Cairns
(Penguin, 2007)

Opera: A Beginner's Guide
Alexandra Wilson
(Oneworld, 2010)

Opera, or, the Undoing of Women
Catherine Clément
(University of Minnesota Press, 1988)

Overture Opera Guides series
(Overture Publishing)

Prima Donna: A History
Rupert Christiansen
(Pimlico, 1995)

The Puccini Problem
Alexandra Wilson
(Cambridge University Press, 2009)

The Queen's Throat: Opera Homosexuality and the Mystery of Desire
Wayne Kostenbaum
(De Capo Press, 2001)

Violetta and her Sisters
Nicholas John
(Faber & Faber, 1994)

WEBSITES

YouTube is a tremendous resource for full operas and excerpts, in video and sound only recordings.
www.youtube.com

An online library of public-domain scores, including operas.
www.imslp.org

The web site of the Metropolitan Opera in New York.
www.metopera.org

The web site of the Royal Opera House in London.
www.roh.org.uk

The Bavarian State Opera web site, offers streaming of live performances of their operas.
www.staatsoper.de

The web site of the Vienna State Opera House in Vienna.
www.wiener-staatsoper.at

The web site of French television channel Mezzo which is devoted to classical music, jazz and world music.
www.mezzo.tv/en

An opera and classical music streaming service which maintains large online libraries, accessible for a fee.
www.medici.tv

EDITOR

Hugo Shirley is Recordings Editor at Gramophone and formerly Deputy Editor of *Opera*. He has been an opera critic for the *Daily Telegraph* and *The Spectator* and is an Honorary Research Fellow in Opera Studies at Oxford Brookes University. He writes widely on opera, has featured on Radio 3 and has published academic articles on Richard Strauss in *The Cambridge Opera Journal*, *Music & Letters* and *The Journal of the Royal Musical Association*.

FOREWORD

Kasper Holten was born in 1973 in Copenhagen, Denmark, and was Director of Opera at the Royal Opera House, Covent Garden, London until 2017. He was artistic director of the Royal Danish Opera from 2000–2011 and headed the opening of Copenhagen's new Opera House in 2005. He has directed more than 70 productions in the UK, Germany, Italy, France, Austria, Scandinavia, Russia, the United States, Japan and Australia, including several world premieres. His production of Wagner's *Ring in Copenhagen* in 2006 won the Gramophone DVD of the Year award. Kasper is also an associate professor at Copenhagen Business School and Vice-President of Opera Europa.

CONTRIBUTORS

John Allison was born in South Africa and studied at the University of Cape Town, where he wrote his PhD thesis on the music of Edward Elgar. He is the editor of the renowned *Opera* magazine and music critic for the *Sunday Telegraph*. He contributes to other publications, including the *Financial Times*, and has written a book on Elgar's sacred music.

Rupert Christiansen has been opera critic for the *Daily Telegraph* since 1996. He is the author of several books on opera, including *Prima Donna* and the *Faber Pocket Guide to Opera*. He also contributes regularly to *Opera* magazine and broadcasts and lectures internationally. Since 2010, he has sat as the British representative on the jury for the €1 million Birgit Nilsson Prize.

George Hall writes widely on classical music and opera in particular for a variety of publications, including *The Guardian*, *The Stage*, *Opera Now* and *BBC Music Magazine*; he is also the UK correspondent of *Opera News* and a member of the board of *Opera*. After taking a degree at the Royal College of Music, he worked as an editor for the *Decca Record Co* for seven years and in a similar capacity for the BBC for twelve. As well as a several opera translations and numerous programme notes and articles, he has also published *The Proms in Pictures* (with Matías Tarnopolsky), and a new English edition of the autobiography of Darius Milhaud (with Christopher Palmer). He has recently contributed articles to the *Overture Opera Guide* series on Le nozze di Figaro, Simon Boccanegra and Carmen.

Cormac Newark studied Music at the University of Oxford, Music Theory and Analysis at King's College London, and orchestral conducting at the École Normale de Musique in Paris. Returning to Oxford, and for three years he was a fellow of Trinity Hall, Cambridge. Between 2002 and 2004 he carried out research funded by the Leverhulme Trust, after which he took up a lectureship at the University of Ulster. He has been the recipient of a number of grants and prizes from, among others, the British Academy, the Worshipful Company of Musicians, the French Government, and the American Musicological Society. His book, *Opera in the Novel from Balzac to Proust*, was published in 2011, and his essays have appeared in *19th-Century Music*, the *Cambridge Opera Journal* and the *Journal of the Royal Musical Association*. He has also written for *Opera* magazine and the *Guardian*.

Anna Picard studied voice and harpsichord at the Royal Academy of Music, London, and with Dr Thomas LoMonaco in New York. She worked in the field of early music before moving into journalism, and was Classical Music Critic of the *Independent on Sunday* from 2000–2012. She now writes for *The Times*, *Opera*, *Opernwelt* and *BBC Music Magazine*, and is a regular contributor to BBC Radio Three. She has written essays and programme notes for English National Opera, Opera North, Opera Holland Park, the Overture Opera Guides (La traviata), the Salzburg Festival, the Lufthansa Festival of Baroque Music and the Royal Concertgebouw Orchestra.

Dr Alexandra Wilson is Reader in Musicology at Oxford Brookes University, where she co-directs the OBERTO opera research unit and teaches undergraduate and postgraduate courses on opera. She has published in many of the leading music journals and is the author of two books: *The Puccini Problem: Opera, Nationalism, and Modernity* and *Opera: A Beginner's Guide*. She has shared her research with a wider public through numerous broadcasts for BBC Radio 3 and via programme essays and talks for opera companies including the Royal Opera, English National Opera, Wexford Festival Opera and Glyndebourne Touring Opera.

INDEX

ACKNOWLEDGEMENTS

PICTURE CREDITS

All reasonable efforts have been made to trace copyright holders and to obtain their permission for the use of copyright material. The publisher apologizes for any errors or omissions in the list below and will gratefully incorporate any corrections in future reprints if notified.

All images from Shutterstock, Inc./www.shutterstock.com and Clipart Images/www.clipart.com unless stated.

2: Lebrecht Music & Arts. 7: Photo By DEA/A. Dagli Orti/DeAgostini/Getty Images. 8: Lebrecht Music & Arts. 9: AKG Images. 11: Lebrecht Music & Arts. 17T: Lebrecht Music & Arts. 17B: AKG Images. 19: Lebrecht Music & Arts. 23L: Didier Contant/Gamma-Rapho via Getty Images. 23R: Library of Congress. 24: Alfredo Dagli Orti/The Art Archive/Corbis. 27: AKG Images. 29: Chris Fredriksson/Alamy. 31T: AKG Images. 31B: Art Media/Print Collector/Getty Images. 37T: DeAgostini/Lebrecht Music & Arts. 37T: Lebrecht Music & Arts. 39T: AKG Images. 39B: Lebrecht Music & Arts. 41: Photo By DEA/A. Dagli Orti/DeAgostini/Getty Images. 45: Library of Congress. 53: Lebrecht Music & Arts. 55BL: Patti Gower/Toronto Star via Getty Images. 55BR: T.Martinot/Lebrecht Music & Arts. 55T: DeAgostini/Getty Images. 57: Lebrecht Music & Arts. 59: The Art Archive/Alamy. 61L: Lebrecht Music & Arts. 62: Library of Congress. 65T: Lebrecht Music & Arts/Tristram Kenton. 67T: Laurie Lewis/Lebrecht Music & Arts. 67L: Laurie Lewis/Lebrecht Music & Arts. 67TR: Caroline P. Digonis/Lebrecht Music & Arts. 73L: Lebrecht Music & Arts. 73R: DeAgostini/Getty Images. 75R: Vincenzo Pinto/AFP/Getty Images. 75L: Lebrecht Music & Arts/Tristram Kenton. 75T: Lebrecht Music & Arts. 77R: V&A Images/Lebrecht Music & Arts. 79BR: FalkensteinFoto/Alamy. 79T: Getty Images. 80: Library of Congress. 83B: Heikki Tuuli/Lebrecht Music & Arts. 83T: Neil Libbert/Lebrecht Music & Arts. 85T: Lebrecht Music & Arts. 85C: Culture-images/Lebrecht Music & Arts. 85B: Lebrecht Music & Arts. 87: Lebrecht Music & Arts. 93R: Lebrecht Music & Arts. 93L: AKG Images/Mauro Pagano. 95: Interfoto/Alamy. 101: Library of Congress. 105BR: Lebrecht Authors. 109TL: DeAgostini/Getty Images. 110: Didier Contant/Gamma-Rapho via Getty Images. 113TL: Lebrecht Music & Arts. 113R: Imagno/Getty Images. 115: Lebrecht Music & Arts. 117: Leemage/Lebrecht Music & Arts. 123T: Leemage/Lebrecht Music & Arts. 123B: Lebrecht Music & Arts. 125T: Lebrecht Music & Arts. 125B: Matti Kolho/Lebrecht Music & Arts. 125R: Lebrecht Music & Arts. 127R: Boris Horvat/AFP/Getty Images. 127L: T.Martinot/Lebrecht Music & Arts. 127T: Lebrecht Music & Arts. 129B: Richard Haughton/Lebrecht Music & Arts. 129TR: Leemage/Lebrecht Music & Arts. 129TL: Lebrecht Music & Arts. 133TL: Chris Stock/Lebrecht Music & Arts. 133TR: Nigel Luckhurst/Lebrecht Music & Arts. 133B: Laurie Lewis/Lebrecht Music & Arts. 135L: Lebrecht Music & Arts. 135R: Library of Congress. 135B: Herbert Gehr/The LIFE Images Collection/Getty Images. 141TL: Lebrecht Music & Arts. 141TR: Interfoto/Alamy. 141B: Interfoto/Alamy. 143T: Library of Congress. 143C: Lebrecht Music & Arts. 145C: Metropolitan Opera Archives/Lebrecht Music & Arts. 145B: Alfred Eisenstaedt/The LIFE Picture Collection/Getty Images. 147B: Colette Masson/Lebrecht Music & Arts. 147TL: Tristram Kenton/Lebrecht Music & Arts. 149T: Lebrecht Music & Arts. 149R: DeAgostini/Lebrecht Music & Arts. 149C: Lebrecht Music & Arts. 151: DPA Picture Alliance Archive/Alamy. 153T: Laurie Lewis/Lebrecht Music & Arts. 153B: Lebrecht Music & Arts.